Corporate Acquisitions and Mergers in India

Corporate Acquisitions and Mergers in India

Fifth Edition

Pradeep Kumar Jain

Singhania & Co, LLP

This book was originally published as a chapter in Corporate Acquisitions and Mergers.

General Editor: Peter Begg

Wolters Kluwer

Published by:
Kluwer Law International B.V.
PO Box 316
2400 AH Alphen aan den Rijn
The Netherlands
E-mail: lrs-sales@wolterskluwer.com
Website: www.wolterskluwer.com/en/solutions/kluwerlawinternational

Sold and distributed by:
Wolters Kluwer Legal & Regulatory U.S.
920 Links Avenue
Landisville, PA 17538
United States of America
E-mail: customer.service@wolterskluwer.com

ISBN 978-94-035-2649-2

e-Book: ISBN 978-94-035-2659-1
web-PDF: ISBN 978-94-035-1260-0

Contents

Singhania & Co, LLP

Mr Pradeep Kumar Jain is a Managing Partner at Singhania & Co LLP, a leading full-service Indian law firm established in 1969. Mr Jain has extensive expertise in the areas of mergers & acquisitions, joint ventures (JVs), corporate laws, maritime laws, financial restructuring laws, infrastructure & project finance and real estate laws. After joining the Firm in 2002, Mr Jain was rapidly promoted to partnership in 2004.

Mr Jain frequently advises clients on matters relating to the development and control regulations, policy and regulatory matters related to foreign investments, foreign exchange controls, foreign technical collaboration, and offers advice in matters related to takeovers, mutual funds, asset management companies, trusteeship, custodianship and foreign institutional investors.

He also appears frequently before arbitral tribunals both in India and outside India (particularly in Singapore, the UK and the USA) to represent the firm's clients in matters related to maritime, contractual and other trade disputes.

Often described as a polymath by his colleagues, Mr Jain is an academic with numerous qualifications. After finishing a bachelor's degree in science, he went on to pursue a Master's degree in Mathematics before applying for a Bachelor's degree in Law and then Master's in Law. Today, Mr Jain is not only a qualified advocate and a member of the Bar Council of India but also an associate member of the Chartered Institute of Securities & Investments. He is also a qualified Company Secretary and a fellow member of the Indian Institute of Company Secretaries of India, member of the London Court of International Arbitration ('LCIA') and Master.

An avid learner himself, Mr Jain follows his passion for academic issues by delivering guest lectures and sharing his thoughts and views on legal issues through articles in various Indian and international publications.

Singhania & Co, LLP

Solicitors & Advocates

International Legal Consultants

83 – C, Mittal Towers, Nariman Point

Mumbai – 400 021

Tel.: +91- 22 2204 9773 / 2285 1011

Fax: +91 – 22 2204 5960

E-mail: pradeepkjain@singhania.net.in

Website: www.singhania.com

List of Abbreviations

ASEAN	Association of Southeast Asian Nations
A.Y	Accounting Year
B2B	Business to Business
CA	Companies Act, 2002
CBEC	Central Board of Excise and Custom
CBDT	Central Board of Direct Taxes
CIR	Committed Information Rates
DGFT	Directorate General of Foreign Trade
DPS	Detailed Public Statement
ECB	External Commercial Borrowing
FFI	Foreign Financial Investor
FDI	Foreign Direct Investment
FEMA	Foreign Exchange Management Act, 1999
FCCB	Foreign Currency Convertible Bonds
FIRC	Foreign Inward Remittance Certificate
FIFP	Foreign Investment Facilitation Portal
FCDR	Foreign Currency Depository Receipts
GAAR	General Anti-Avoidance Rule
GDP	Gross Domestic Product
GST	Goods & Service Tax
IAA	Impermissible Avoidance Agreement
IBC	Insolvency & Bankruptcy Code
INR	Indian Currency
ITA	Income Tax Act, 1961
ITES	Information Technology Enabled Service
IPP	Institutional Placement Programme

JV	Joint Venture
LODR	Listing Obligation and Disclosure Requirements
MCA	Ministry of Corporate Affairs
MRTP	Monopolies & Restrictive Trade Practices
NBFC	Non-Banking Financial Company
NCLT	National Company Law Tribunal
NCLAT	National Company Law Appellate Tribunal
NOC	No Objection Certificate
NRO	Non-resident Ordinary
NRE	Non-resident External
NRI	Non-resident Indian
OPC	One Person Company
PIO	Person of Indian Origin
PAC	Person Acting in Concert
PA	Public Announcement
PSU	Public Sector Undertaking
PSE	Public Sector Enterprises
RBI	Reserve Bank of India
ROC	Registrar of Companies
STT	Securities Transaction Tax
SAFTA	South Asian Free Trade Area
SEBI	Securities Exchange Board of India
TDRs	Transferable Development Rights
WTO	World Trade Organization

Important Links

01.	The National Portal of India	www.india.gov.in
02.	The Reserve Bank of India	www.rbi.org.in
03.	The Ministry of Corporate Affairs	www.mca.gov.in
04.	The Ministry of Finance	www.finmin.gov.in
05.	The Insurance Regulatory Authority of India ('IRDA')	www.irdai.gov.in
06.	The Pension Fund Regulatory and Development Authority	www.pfrda.org.in
07.	Department of Industrial Policy and Promotion	www.dipp.nic.in
08.	SEBI Investor Awareness Website	https://investor.sebi.gov.in/
09.	Serious Fraud Investigation Office	www.sfio.nic.in
10.	Ministry of Labour & Employment	www.labour.nic.in
11.	National Company Law Tribunal	https://nclt.gov.in/
12.	The Securities Board Exchange of India	www.sebi.gov.in
13.	The Bombay Stock Exchange	www.bseindia.com
14.	The National Stock Exchange of India	www.nseindia.com
15.	The Foreign Investment Facilitation Portal	www.FIFP.gov.in

1 INDIA CALLING: A LAND OF OPPORTUNITY FOR BUSINESS

1.1 Introduction

[01] India has already marked its presence as one of the fastest-growing economies in the world. It has been ranked among the top three most attractive destinations for inbound investments. Since 1991, the regulatory environment in terms of foreign investment has been consistently eased to make it investor-friendly. Apart from being a critical driver of economic growth, foreign direct investment (FDI) is a major source of non-debt financial resources for the economic development of India. Foreign companies invest in India to take advantage of cheaper wages, as well as special investment privileges such as exemptions. For a country where foreign investments are being made, it also means the acquisition of technical know-how and generation of employment. The continuous inflow of FDI into India, which is now allowed across several industries, clearly shows the faith that overseas investors have in the country's economy.

[02] The Indian government's policy regime and a robust business environment have ensured that foreign capital keeps flowing into the country. The government has taken many initiatives in recent years, such as relaxing FDI norms across sectors such as defence, Public Sector Undertaking (PSU) oil refineries, telecoms, power exchanges and stock exchanges, and Public Sector Enterprises (PSE), among others. FDI is usually preferred over other forms of external finance because it is non-debt creating, and non-volatile, and its returns depend on the performance of the projects financed by the investors. It also facilitates international trade and the transfer of knowledge, skills and technology. FDI includes mergers and acquisitions, building new facilities, reinvesting profits earned from overseas operations and intracompany loans.

1.2 Country Profile

[03] India, officially the Republic of India (*Bhārat Gaṇarājya*), is a country in South Asia. It is the seventh-largest country by area, the second-most populous country with over 1.3 bn people, and the most populous democracy in the world. Bounded by the Indian Ocean on the south and southwest, and by the Bay of Bengal on the southeast, it shares land borders with Pakistan to the west, China, Nepal, and Bhutan to the northeast, and Burma (Myanmar) and Bangladesh to the east. In the Indian Ocean, Sri Lanka and the Maldives are in close vicinity; in addition, India's Andaman and Nicobar Islands share a maritime border with Thailand and Indonesia.

[04] There are several languages in India, the major ones being the Indo-Aryan languages spoken by 75% of Indians and the Dravidian languages spoken by southern Indians. Other languages spoken in India belong to the Austro-Asiatic, Tibeto-Burman, a few minor language families and isolates. More than three millennia of language contact has led to significant mutual influence among the four predominant language families in mainland India and South Asia. The Constitution of India does not give any language the status of a national language. The official languages of the Union Government of the Republic of India are Hindi in the Devanagari script and English. The Eighth Schedule of the Indian Constitution lists twenty-two languages, which have been referred to as scheduled languages and are given recognition, status and official encouragement. In addition, the Government of India has awarded the distinction of 'classical language' to Tamil, Sanskrit, Odia, Kannada, Telugu and Malayalam. According to the Census of India of 2001, India has 122 major languages and 1 599 other languages.

[05] The Indian landmass contains a multitude of both types of resources, i.e., minerals and agricultural, and its economy, especially in rural areas, is heavily dependent on their consumption or export. India has a large proportion of well-watered fertile lands. In the alluvial soil of the Northern Great Plains of the Sutlej-Ganga plains and the Brahmaputra Valley wheat, rice, maize, sugarcane, jute, cotton, rapeseed, mustard, sesame, linseed, etc., are grown in abundance. Hills, mountains and less fertile lands are put under pasture. Scientific methods are followed in rearing cattle. India maintains a rich diversity of domestic animals. Diverse agro-climatic conditions in India facilitate the cultivation of a large number of horticulture crops such as vegetables, fruits, flowers, medicinal and aromatic plants, mushrooms, etc., and plantation crops like tea, coffee and rubber. India possesses a variety of natural vegetation since the country has a varied relief and climate. Its forests are confined to the plateaus and hilly mountainous areas. India has a great variety of fauna. There are many national parks and hundreds of wildlife sanctuaries.

[06] The Rupee, or, more specifically, the Indian Rupee, is the official currency of the Republic of India. The issuance of the currency is controlled by the Reserve Bank of India (RBI).

[07] Labour is the pillar of the economy of India. In 2012, there were around 487 million workers, the second-largest total after China. Of these, over 94% work in unincorporated, unorganized enterprises ranging from pushcart vendors to home-based diamond and gem polishing operations. The organized sector includes workers employed by the government, state-owned enterprises and private-sector enterprises. In 2008, the organized sector employed over 27.5 million workers, of which 17.3 million worked for the government or government-owned entities.

[08] Infrastructure is largely responsible for propelling India's overall development. The industry enjoys intense focus from the top officials of the Government for initiating policies that would ensure the creation of world-class infrastructure in the country on time. This sector includes power, bridges, dams, roads and urban infrastructure development. Since the economic liberalization of the 1990s, infrastructure development has progressed rapidly; today, there are a variety of modes of transport by land, water and air. Public transport remains the primary mode of transport for most of the population, and India's public transport systems are among the most heavily used in the world. India's rail network is the fourth-longest and the most heavily used system in the world.

1.3 Government and Political System

[09] India is a stable democracy, so there is virtually no risk of the country failing. Even if the ruling party or leader changes, most business-related laws and policies generally maintain continuity, especially since liberalization. Hence it offers the political stability that is vital to foreign investments. Government agencies, which have a pro-business attitude, work closely with the business sector to promote economic growth. Businesses can also tap into their developed capital markets as an alternative source of financing. The FDI regime has also been progressively liberalized during the course of the 1990s (particularly after 2000). A number of restrictions on foreign investment have been removed, and procedures have been simplified. With limited exceptions, foreign nationals and entities incorporated outside India can invest directly in India, either on their own or as a joint venture (JV) in those industries where foreign investment is restricted. Moreover, investment ceilings, which are applicable in certain cases, are gradually being removed/ phased out.

[10] India has witnessed a steady increase in foreign inflows over the years. FDI net inflows have grown at a rate of over 30% compounded annually over the last decade. Its financial system is well-regulated and offers a broad range of services, including banking, insurance, asset management and treasury services. Businesses here can easily tap into their deep and liquid capital markets as an alternative source to raise funds. Trade associations of which India is an important member include the South Asian Free Trade Agreement (SAFTA), the Association of Southeast Asian Nations (ASEAN) and the World Trade Organization (WTO)

1.4 Supremacy of the Constitution and Separation of Powers

[11] The Constitution of India is the supreme law of the Republic of India, and no legislation is allowed, which conflicts with/is inconsistent with the basic structure of the Constitution. The Republic of India is divided into various states and union territories. One of the essential features of the Constitution of India is the division of powers. It has clearly defined powers between the Union and the States and divides them into the following three lists:

1.	Union List	ninety-seven subjects
2.	State List	sixty-six subjects
3.	Concurrent List	forty-seven subjects

[12] As regards the subjects contained in the first two lists, only parliament and the respective state assemblies can make laws, while in the case of subjects contained in the third list, both can make laws. The Supreme Court of India is the ultimate authority to interpret the Constitution and can declare any law unconstitutional. It is also a National Company Law Tribunal (NCLT) of law to hear disputes between the Union Government and the States Governments.

1.5 Legal System

[13] The legal and judicial system in India is robust and efficient. Thus businesses can count on India's rigorous enforcement of the law. The Indian judiciary has a reputation for being independent and non-partisan. Judges are not appointed on political considerations. They enjoy a high standing in society. The judicial system has a unified structure. Under Article 141 of the Constitution of India, the law declared by the Supreme NCLT will be binding on all NCLTs in the territory of India. The Supreme NCLT, the NCLTs, and the lower NCLTs constitute a single Judiciary. Broadly, there is a three-tier division. The influence of the British Judicial System continues to be significant. The official language for NCLT proceedings in the NCLT and the Supreme NCLT is English. The procedural law for land, as well as most of the commercial and corporate laws, is modelled on English laws. English case law is often referred to and relied upon, both by lawyers and judges. Law enforcement in India is conducted by numerous law enforcement agencies. At the Union (federal) level, the agencies are part of the Union Ministry of Home Affairs and support the states in their duties. While the federal nature of the Constitution in India means that much law is issued at a Union level, the bulk of the policing lies with the respective states and territories of India. Contractual obligations are regularized by the Indian Contract Act, 1872 and the Specific Relief Act, 1963. These govern entry into contractual relations, the execution of contracts, and the effects of breach of contracts.

1.6 Current Economic Aspects

[14] The economy of India is the sixth largest in the world by nominal Gross Domestic Product (GDP) and the third-largest by purchasing power parity. The Indian economy expanded 7.3% in the year ended March 2015, in line with the initial forecast and marginally higher than the 6.9% recorded in the previous year. GDP rose 7.5% in January-March 2015 compared with 6.7%. Cross-border deals have dominated the Indian M&A landscape and, on an aggregate basis over the last decade, constituted almost two-thirds of total announced M&A transactions in India. According to the 2015 India Technology Product M&A Industry Report, M&A activity will continue to accelerate. Domestic transactions will dominate the E-Commerce and Consumer Internet sectors, while cross-border M&A will dominate Business to Business (B2B)/Enterprise Software transactions, and the acquisition of B2C companies in selected sectors.

1.7 Main Industries

[15] The key sectors or industries in India are automotive, aerospace and defence, engineering and machinery, chemical industries, transportation, the Information Technology (IT) & Information Technology Enabled Service (ITES) industry, and real estate. Foreign investment in India requires approval, but certain types of investment qualify for automatic approval. Up to 100% foreign ownership may be permitted, except in certain cases. All sectors open to private investment are open to foreign investors as well, although the mandatory approval requirement for foreign investment, granted on a discretionary basis, acts as a restriction. For certain specified telecommunications services, the government has allowed 49% under the automatic route and 100% under the approval route. While informal guidelines have been formulated in certain sectors (such as financial services and mining) where the government increased the limit up to 100%, nevertheless such limits can be revised by the Governments due to changes in the world economy and therefore investors are advised to obtain local professional advice. Private Equity (PE) has emerged as an important source of stable equity capital in India. Companies of all sizes ranging from early-stage to large corporates have attracted capital from PEs. As the growth of the Indian economy has maintained a steady pace, industry-wide consolidations are an attractive route for a PE investor to make an exit.

1.8 Liberalized FDI Regime: Red Carpet Welcome for Investors

[16] India is one of the most liberal countries in terms of its FDI regime, as over 90% of the sectors fall under the automatic route. Under the automatic route, no approval from the government or RBI is required to set up business in India. Foreign Investment in India is governed by the Foreign Exchange Management Act 1999 (FEMA). The nodal agency for all foreign investment is the RBI, the Central Bank. Foreign investment in India is only prohibited in areas like agriculture, atomic energy, defence, gambling, betting, lottery, trading in Transferable Development Rights (TDRs) and retail (except Single Brand Retailing, in which investment is permitted up to 100% under the automatic route.

1.9 Honest and Transparent System: Only Way to Attract Business

[17] The discourse over the costs of business in India has been preoccupied with two particular elements: The macro problem of inflation and the micro problem of dealing with corruption. However, various reforms have been adopted, and strategies are evolving to counter these rising costs. Enactment of statutes, like the Right

to Information Act and the Citizen Charters, are some of the steps taken by the Parliament. The reformers have been so keen to develop infrastructure in which foreign investors will feel at home, that little attention has been paid to the costs of that infrastructure. This high-cost infrastructure has typically been concentrated in a few cities. India offers a highly-rated human capital base recognized for its skills, knowledge and talent at a comparatively low cost. At the same time, the workers, who are generally very enthusiastic about their work, are also big-hearted consumers who do not mind buying the most expensive brands in the world.

2 MERGERS & ACQUISITIONS

2.1 Introduction

[18] Due to globalization, liberalization, technological developments and the resultant intensely competitive business environment, cross-border mergers and acquisitions ('M&A') have become very popular throughout the world in recent times. M&A transactions have historically been the favourite tool used by companies for restructuring their businesses.

2.2 Meaning of Merger, Takeover and Acquisition, Amalgamation

2.2.1 Merger

[19] A merger is a combination of two companies into one company where one company loses its identity. It is an arrangement whereby the assets of two companies become vested under the control of one company. A merger arises when two firms, often of about the same size, agree to go forward as a single new company rather than remain separately owned and operated.

2.2.2 Takeover/Acquisition

[20] Takeover/Acquisition is a growth strategy in which one company acquires all the shares (or all the assets and liabilities) of another company. When one company takes over another company and clearly establishes itself as the new owner, the purchase is called an acquisition.

[21] There is no tangible difference between an acquisition and a takeover. The word takeover is more conventionally used in the context of takeovers of public companies. However, both words can be used interchangeably – the only difference being that each word carries a slightly different connotation. Typically, the takeover is used to refer to a hostile takeover where the company being acquired is resisting. In contrast, the term acquisition is frequently used to describe more friendly acquisitions, or used in conjunction with the word merger, where both companies are willing to join together. The Companies Act, 2013 provides a complete code in relation to takeovers of shares of a public company. And if the company to be acquired is listed on the stock market the provisions of the Securities Exchange Board of India Act (SEBI) (Substantial Acquisition of Shares and Takeovers (SAST)) Regulation need to be followed strictly.

2.2.3 Amalgamation

[22] Amalgamation means the bringing together of two or more businesses into a single entity. In other words, amalgamation means combining two or more undertakings into a single undertaking. In this type of amalgamation, two or more companies come together to form a new company, and the combining companies lose their individual identities.

2.3 Cross-Border Mergers

[23] A cross-border merger is a transaction in which the assets and operations of two firms belonging to or registered in two different countries are combined to establish a new legal entity. In a cross-border acquisition, control of the relevant assets and operations is transferred from a local to a foreign company, with the former becoming an affiliate of the latter.

2.4 Main Motive for the Increase in Mergers and Acquisitions

[24] For most companies, profit growth is their priority, and they are prepared to take significant measures to achieve this objective. The most popular motive behind many cross-border M&A transactions is to increase a company's efficiency in production. Merging companies within the same industry allows companies to increase their scale of production.

[25] Mergers and acquisitions are usually aimed at maximizing shareholder value by enhancing production and marketing operations. The primary objective is usually to gain market share, expand the customer base, cut competition, or enter into a new market or product segment.

2.5 Other Driving Forces for Cross-Border Mergers and Acquisitions

[26] Other driving forces for Cross-Border M&A transactions include:

(1) Geographical diversification.
(2) Technology sharing and innovation to reduce cost.

(3) Market pressures and falling demand due to international competition.
(4) The quest for new market opportunities.
(5) Globalization of markets.

2.6 Different Categories/Types of Mergers

[27] *Merger* is the combination of two or more companies that can be merged together either by way of amalgamation or absorption. The combining of two or more companies is generally effected by offering to stockholders of one company securities in the acquiring company in exchange for the surrender of their stock. Mergers may fall within (any one or a combination of) the following categories.

2.6.1 Horizontal Merger

[28] This is a merger of two or more companies that compete in the same industry. It is a merger with a direct competitor and thus expands the firm's operations in the same industry. Horizontal mergers are designed to achieve economies of scale and reduce the number of competitors in the industry.

2.6.2 Vertical Merger

[29] This is a merger that takes place through the combination of two companies operating in the same industry but at different stages of production or distribution. If a company takes over its supplier/producer of raw materials, then this is said to result in 'backward integration' of its activities. However, 'forward integration' results where a manufacturing company decides to acquire a retailer or customer company. Vertical mergers provide the means to achieve total integration for those firms striving for ownership of all phases of the production cycle, including the marketing network.

2.6.3 Co-generic Merger

[30] This is a type of merger, where two companies in the same or related industries are offering related but not identical products and which may achieve enhanced benefits from similar distribution channels. The potential benefit from these mergers is high because these transactions offer opportunities to diversify around a common set of strategic resources.

2.6.4 Conglomerate Merger

[31] These mergers involve firms engaged in unrelated activities. In other words, the businesses of the two companies are not related to each other either horizontally or vertically. In a pure conglomerate, there are no significant common factors between the companies involved, whether in terms of production, marketing, research and development, or technology. Conglomerate mergers are mergers of different kinds of businesses under a single flagship company. Possible purposes of such mergers include the utilization of financial resources, enlarged debt capacity and possible synergies of managerial functions. They do not have a direct impact on the acquisition of monopoly power and are thus generally of no concern to competition authorities.

2.7 Parameters to Evaluate M&A Transactions

[32] Not every merger is successful. The factors which are required to measure the success of any merger are briefly discussed below:

(1) The earning performance of the merged company can be measured by return on total assets and return on net worth. Simple vertical and horizontal mergers have generally been found to be more successful by industry, whereas the performance of conglomerate mergers tends to be more variable.
(2) Whether the merged companies yield a larger net profit in combination than the sum of their individual net profits did before, whether they yield a higher return on total funds employed, and/or whether the merged entity is better able to sustain the increase in earnings.
(3) Success or failure is ultimately determined by the market capitalization of the merged entity as well as by its dividend rate and distributions.
(4) Whether the merged company is creating a larger business organization more capable of survival and/or which provides a better basis for growth.
(5) Comparison of the performance of the merged company with the performance of similar-sized companies in the same business in respect of:
   (a) sales;
   (b) return on assets;
   (c) net profits;
   (d) earnings per share;
   (e) market price per share.

[33] In general, growth in profits, an increase in dividend payouts, and an increase in size providing an improved basis for future growth are also factors that help to determine the success or failure of a merged company.

3 THE REGULATORY FRAMEWORK FOR MERGERS AND AMALGAMATIONS

3.1 Applicable Statutes

[34] The main statutes which constitute the regulatory framework for mergers and amalgamations include:

(1) The Companies Act, 2013.
(2) The Companies (Compromise, Arrangements and Amalgamations) Rules, 2016.
(3) The NCLT Rules, 2016.
(4) Exchange Control Regulations.
(5) The FEMA.
(6) The Securities Exchange Board of India Act, 1992 ('SEBI').
(7) The Income Tax Act, 1961 (ITA)
(8) Stock Exchanges and Listing Agreements.
(9) The Indian Stamp Act, 1899 and various States' Stamp Acts.
(10) Double Taxation Avoidance Agreements ('DTAA').
(11) The Competition Act, 2002 (CA).
(12) The SEBI (Listing Obligations and Disclosure Requirements) Regulations, 2015.
(13) FDI Policy.
(14) IBC Code 2016.

3.2 Regulators & Authorities

[35] The principal regulators and authorities governing the conduct of such transactions are:

(1) The NCLTs of various jurisdictions.
(2) The RBI.
(3) The Foreign Investment Promotion Board.
(4) The Registrar of Companies (ROC) under the Ministry of Corporate Affairs ('MCA').
(5) The Central Board of Direct Tax ('CBDT').
(6) The Central Board of Excise & Customs ('CBEC').
(7) The Securities Exchange Board of India ('SEBI').
(8) The Directorate General of Foreign Trade (DGFT).
(9) Local Authorities.
(10) Other Ministries and authorities depending upon the particular business sector of the relevant company.
(11) The 'NCLT' and National Company Law Appellate Tribunal ('NCLAT').
(12) The Goods and Service Tax Council.

4 CHOICES OF ACQUISITION VEHICLE

4.1 Different Modes of Acquisition for Foreign Purchasers

[36] A foreign purchaser has a number of different vehicles available to him for the acquisition of business entities in India. Set out below is a list of different modes of acquisition that a foreign purchaser can utilize;

4.1.1 Local Holding Company

[37] At a broad level, any indirect foreign investment (through an Indian company or companies) is not construed as a foreign investment where the intermediate Indian holding company is owned and/or controlled by resident Indians. The criteria for determining the ownership and control of an Indian company are ownership of more than 50% of the shares, along with control of the governing board. Downstream investments made by Indian entities are not taken into account in determining whether these criteria are met. Earlier, dividends in India were subject to a dividend distribution tax. However, effective from 1 April 2020 domestic companies are no longer required to deduct DDT and the dividend is taxable in the hands of the shareholders.

4.1.2 Foreign Parent Company

[38] Foreign investors may invest directly through the foreign parent company, subject to the prescribed foreign investment guidelines.

4.1.3 Non-resident Intermediate Holding Company

[39] An intermediate holding company resident in another territory could be used for investment into India, in order to minimize the tax leakage in India through, for example, withholdings at source and capital gains taxes on exit. This may allow the purchaser to take advantage of a more favourable tax treaty with India. However, *evidence of substance* of the intermediate holding company in its home jurisdiction is required.

4.1.4 Local Branch

[40] According to the guidelines prescribed by the RBI, a foreign company is not permitted to use a local branch In the form of a liaison office for acquiring Indian assets. However, a branch office (BO) and a project office (PO) can acquire property for their own use to carry out permitted/incidental activities but not for leasing or renting out the property. However, entities from Pakistan, Bangladesh, Sri Lanka, Afghanistan, Iran, Nepal, Bhutan, China, Hong Kong and Macau require prior approval from the Reserve Bank to acquire immovable property in India for a BO/PO.

4.1.5 Joint Ventures

[41] JVs are normally used where specific sectoral caps are applicable under the foreign investment guidelines. In such scenarios, a JV with an Indian partner is established that will subsequently acquire the Indian target. In planning a JV, the current guidelines for calculating indirect foreign investments should be considered.

4.2 Assets Purchase

[42] In cases where an acquiring company is uncertain about ongoing disputes, their magnitude, or their future implications, then it may prefer to acquire individual assets of the company for fixed consideration.

[43] In this context, a 'Slump Sale' is a transfer of one or more undertakings for a lump sum consideration without values being assigned to the individual assets and liabilities acquired.

4.3 Share Purchase

[44] The acquiring company may acquire an Indian company by way of purchase of its shares, either directly from the promoters, if the company is a closely held company, or on a stock market if the company is listed there, with or without the consent of the promoters group.

4.4 Foreign Collaborations and Investment

[45] There are four main types of foreign collaboration:

(1) Financial collaboration (foreign equity participation) where only the provision of foreign equity is involved.
(2) Technical collaboration (technology transfer) involving the licensing of technology by the foreign collaborator in exchange for due compensation.
(3) Marketing collaboration is an arrangement whereby the foreign collaborator agrees to market the products of the domestic company in the international market. The purpose of marketing collaboration is to create value for customers, build strong customer relationships and promote exports.
(4) Consultancy collaboration is where a consultant provides professional advice in a particular area of expertise such as management, accountancy, human resources (HR), marketing or finance. Consultancy collaboration is an arrangement whereby the foreign company bridges the information gap by agreeing to provide managerial skills and expertise to the domestic company.

5 TAX LAWS

5.1 Introduction: Tax Laws

[46] In recent years, India has experienced a sharp rise in M&A activity, including outbound as well as inbound activity, owing to its dominant participation in the global economy. These activities are subject to the interplay of various tax and regulatory regimes, ranging from direct and indirect taxation to securities laws, company laws, foreign exchange control regulations, competition laws and stamp duty laws. The various provisions of tax law applicable to cross-border M&A transactions are explained below

5.2 General Anti-Avoidance Rules

[47] General Anti-Avoidance Rules (GAAR) came into force on 1 April 2018. GAAR provisions are applicable only if tax benefits arising for all parties to the arrangement exceed INR30 m in the relevant financial year. The GAAR empowers the Tax Authority to declare an 'arrangement' entered into by an assessee to be an '*Impermissible Avoidance Agreement' (IAA)*, resulting in a denial of the tax benefit under the provisions of the relevant Act or tax treaty. An IAA is an arrangement the main purpose of which is to obtain a tax benefit and which:

(1) Creates rights and obligations that are not ordinarily created between persons dealing at arm's length.
(2) Results in the misuse or abuse of tax provisions.
(3) Lacks commercial substance.
(4) Is not for a bona fide person.

5.3 Taxability of Indirect Share Transfers

[48] Where a foreign company transfers shares of another foreign company to a third company, and the value of those shares is derived substantially from assets situated in India, then any capital gains derived from the transfer are subject to income tax in India. Further, payment for such shares is subject to Indian withholding tax (WHT), and the buyer (including a non-resident buyer) is required to withhold tax at applicable rates on the payment or accrual of consideration payable to a non-resident. No withholding of tax is required for the acquisition of shares from Indian residents.

5.4 Taxation on Acquisition of an Indian Company by a Foreign Entity

[49] The acquisition of the business of an Indian company can be accomplished by the purchase of shares or by the purchase of all or some of its assets. From a tax perspective, long-term capital gains arising on a sale of equity shares through any of the recognized stock exchanges in India are exempt from tax, provided securities transaction tax (STT) is paid. All other gains on the sales of assets are potentially taxable. In some cases (in addition to capital gains taxes), other transfer taxes, such as stamp duty, may also be levied.

5.5 Determination of Purchase Price

[50] The cost of an asset for tax purposes is generally regarded as its actual cost. However, this general rule may be subject to a degree of variability depending on the nature of the particular asset and of the particular transaction:

(1) An appropriate allocation of the purchase price by the buyer in the case of acquisition by means of a slump sale is critical from a tax perspective where the entire business undertaking is transferred as a going concern for a lump sum consideration. The tax authorities normally accept the allocation of the purchase price on a fair value basis or on some other reasonable commercial basis. Reports from independent valuation providers are also acceptable.
(2) For sale transactions where the cost of individual assets is itemized, the cost paid by the acquirer as agreed may be accepted as the acquisition cost, subject to certain conditions. Therefore, under both slump sales and itemized sales, a step-up in the cost base of the assets may be obtained.

5.6 Goodwill

[51] Under Indian tax law, only the depreciation/amortization of intangible assets, such as know-how, patents, copyrights, trademarks, licenses and franchises, or any similar business or commercial rights, is permissible. Therefore, when an excess of consideration over the value of the assets arises because of such intangible assets, a depreciation allowance may be available. Recent judicial precedents have allowed depreciation on goodwill arising out of amalgamation by treating it as a depreciable asset under the Income Tax Act.

5.7 Depreciation

[52] Depreciation charged in the accounts is ignored for tax purposes. The tax laws provide for specific tax depreciation rates for the tangible assets (buildings, machinery, plant or furniture), depending on the nature of the asset used in the business. Depreciation is allowed on a 'block of assets' basis. All assets of similar nature are classified under a single block, and any additions/deletions are made directly against the block. The depreciation rates apply on a reducing-balance basis on the entire block. (However, companies engaged in the generation and/or distribution of power have the option to claim tax depreciation on a straight-line basis). In the first year, if the assets are used in the business for less than 180 days, only half of the entire eligible depreciation for that year is deductible. When the assets are used for more than 180 days in the first year, the entire eligible depreciation for that year is allowed. Capital allowances are available for certain types of assets, such as assets used in scientific research or other specified businesses, subject to certain conditions.

5.8 Tax Attributes

[53] Accrued tax losses cannot usually be transferred regardless of the method of acquisition used. However, certain tax benefits/deductions that are available to an undertaking may be available to the acquirer when the undertaking as a whole is transferred as a going concern as a result of a slump sale. In circumstances where there are pending proceedings against the transferor, the tax authorities have the power to claim any tax on account of completion of such proceedings from the transferee where the transfer is made for inadequate consideration.

5.9 GST Provisions on Mergers and Acquisitions

[54] The Goods and Services Tax ('GST') is an indirect tax introduced in India on 1 July 2017, and which is applicable throughout India. It, therefore, replaces various statutes like the Central Sales Tax Act, States Sales Tax Act, Value Added Tax, Excise Act, etc., of the Central Government and State Governments. It also affects some companies planning M&A transactions due to the definition of 'supply' in the Central Goods and Services Act ('CGST').

Section 7(1) of CGST defines 'supply' to mean and include:

(a) all forms of supply of goods or services or both such as sale, transfer, barter, exchange, license, rental, lease, or disposal made or agreed to be made for a consideration by a person in the course or furtherance of business.

[(aa) the activities or transactions, by a person, other than an individual, to its members or constituents or vice-versa, for cash, deferred payment or other valuable consideration.Explanation – For the purposes of this clause, it is hereby clarified that, notwithstanding anything contained in any other law for the time being in force or any judgment, decree or order of any Court, tribunal or authority, the person and its members or constituents shall be deemed to be two separate persons and the supply of activities or transactions *inter se* shall be deemed to take place from one such person to another;]

(b) import of services for a consideration whether or not in the course or furtherance of business;

(c) the activities specified in Schedule I of the Act made or agreed to be made without consideration;

(d) the activities to be treated as a supply of goods or supply of services as referred to in Schedule II of the Act; and

(1A) '*where certain activities or transactions constitute a supply in accordance with the provisions of sub-section (1), they shall be treated either as supply of goods or supply of services as referred to in Schedule II.*'

Section 7(2) of CGST states that notwithstanding anything contained in subsection (1):

(a) activities or transactions specified in Schedule III [of the Act]; or
(b) such activities or transactions undertaken by the Central Government, a State Government or any local authority in which they are engaged as public authorities, as may be notified by the Government on the recommendations of the Council, shall be treated neither as a supply of goods nor a supply of services.

[55] According to Schedule I of CGST, the following activities shall be treated as a supply; even if made without consideration:

(1) The permanent transfer or disposal of business assets where input tax credit has been made available on those assets.
(2) The supply of goods or services or both between related persons or between distinct persons as specified in section 25 of the Act, when made in the course or furtherance of business: Provided that gifts not exceeding INR50 000 in value in a financial year by an employer to an employee shall not be treated either as a supply of goods or of services.
(3) The supply of goods- (a) by a principal to his agent where the agent undertakes to supply such goods on behalf of the principal; or (b) by an agent to his principal where the agent undertakes to receive such goods on behalf of the principal.
(4) The import of services by a person from a related person or from any of his other establishments outside India, in the course or furtherance of business.

[56] According to Schedule II of CGST, the following transfer of business assets shall be treated as a supply:

(1) Where goods forming part of the assets of a business are transferred or disposed of by or under the directions of the person carrying on the business so as no longer to form part of those assets, whether or not for a consideration, such transfer or disposal is a supply of goods by that person.
(2) Where, by or under the direction of a person carrying on a business, goods held or used for the purposes of the business are put to any private use or are used, or made available to any person for use, for any purpose other than a purpose of the business, whether or not for a consideration, the usage or making available of such goods is a supply of services.
(3) Where any person ceases to be a taxable person, then any goods forming part of the assets of any business carried on by him shall be deemed to be supplied by him in the course or furtherance of his business immediately before he ceases to be a taxable person, unless: (i) the business is transferred as a going concern to another person; or (ii) the business is carried on by a personal representative who is deemed to be a taxable person.

5.9.1 Transfer of Credit

[57] Section 18(3) states that where there is a change in the constitution of a registered person on account of the sale, merger, demerger, amalgamation, lease or transfer of a business, with specific provisions for the transfer of liabilities of the business, the [registered person] shall be allowed to transfer the input tax credit which remains unutilized in his electronic credit ledger to such sold, merged, demerged, amalgamated, leased or transferred business in such manner as is prescribed under rule 41 of CGST Rules 2017.

5.9.2 Liability in Case of Amalgamation or Merger of Companies

[58] When two or more companies are amalgamated or merged in pursuance of an order of NCLT or of a Tribunal or otherwise, and the order is to take effect from a date earlier than the date of the order and any two or more of such companies have supplied or received any goods or services or both to or from each other during the period commencing on the date from which the order takes effect until the date of the order, then such transactions of supply and receipt must be included in the turnover of supply or receipt of the respective companies and they shall be liable to pay tax accordingly.

[59] Notwithstanding anything contained in the order, for the purposes of the Act, the said two or more companies would be treated as distinct companies for the period up to the date of the said order, and the registration certificates of the said companies will be cancelled with effect from the date of the said order.

5.10 Transfer Taxes

[60] The transfer of assets by way of a slump sale attracts stamp duty. Stamp duty implications differ from state to state. Rates generally range from 5% to 10% for immovable property and from 3% to 5% for movable property, usually based on the amount of consideration received for the transfer or the market value of the property transferred (whichever is higher). Depending on the nature of the assets transferred, appropriate structuring of the transfer mechanics may reduce the overall stamp duty cost.

5.11 Taxability on Sale of a Business by Way of Sale of Shares

[61] The following rules apply in relation to the taxation of capital gains arising from a sale of shares:

(1) The sale of shares is taxed on the actual capital gains to the seller without any deduction for any difference between the underlying net asset values and the consideration paid.
(2) When shares are held by the seller for twelve months or less, the gains are characterized as short-term capital gains and are subject to tax at the following rates:
  (a) 33.3840% for a domestic company whose total income is between INR1 crore–INR10 crore;
  (b) 34.9440% for a domestic company whose total income exceeds INR10 crores;
  (c) 42.4320% for a foreign company whose total income is between INR1 crore–INR10 crores;
  (d) 43.6800% for a foreign company whose total income exceeds INR10 crores;
  (e) 34.3200% (flat rate) for a Foreign Financial Investor ('FFI') whose total income is between INR1 crore–INR10 crores;
  (f) 35.8800% (flat rate) for a Foreign Financial Investor ('FFI') whose total income exceeds INR10 crores.
(3) If the transaction is subject to Securities Transactions Tax ('STT'), short-term capital gains arising on transfers of equity shares are taxed at the following rates:
  (a) 16.6920% for a domestic company whose total income is between INR1 crore–INR10 crores;
  (b) 17.4720% for a domestic company whose total income exceeds INR10 crores;
  (c) 15.9120% for a foreign company whose total income is between INR1 crore–INR10 crores;
  (d) 16.3800% for a foreign company whose total income exceeds INR10 crores;
  (e) 17.1600% for a Foreign Financial Investor ('FFI') whose total income is between INR1 crore–INR10 crores;
  (f) 17.9400% for a Foreign Financial Investor ('FFI') whose total income exceeds INR10 crores.
(4) Where the shares have been held for more than twelve months, the gains are characterized as long-term capital gains and are subject to tax as follows:
  (a) If the transaction is not subject to STT:
    (i) 22.2560% for a domestic company whose total income is between INR1 crore – INR10 crores.
    (ii) 23.2960% for a domestic company whose total income exceeds INR10 crores.
    (iii) 21.2160% for a foreign company whose total income is between INR1 crore – INR10 crores.
    (iv) 21.8400% for a foreign company whose total income exceeds INR10 crores.
    (v) 22.8800% for a Foreign Financial Investor ('FFI') whose total income is between INR1 crore – INR10 crores.

(vi) 23.9200% for a Foreign Financial Investor ('FFI') whose total income exceeds INR10 crores.

(vii) A concessionary rate of 10.6080% applies to the transfer of capital assets in the form of unlisted securities in the hands of non-residents (including foreign companies) where total income is between INR1 crore – INR10 crores. The concessionary rate must be applied to capital gains without the benefit of exchange fluctuation and indexation.

(viii) A concessionary rate of 10.9200% applies to the transfer of capital assets in the form of unlisted securities in the hands of non-residents (including foreign companies) where total income exceeds INR10 crores. The concessionary rate must be applied to capital gains without the benefit of exchange fluctuation and indexation.

(5) If the transactions are subject to STT, long-term capital gains arising on the transfer of equity shares are exempt from tax.

5.12 Tax Losses

[62] Tax losses consist of normal business losses and unabsorbed tax depreciation (where there is insufficient income to absorb the current-year depreciation). Both types of losses are eligible for carry forward and are thus available for the purchaser. Business tax losses can be carried forward for a period of eight years and offset against future profits. Unabsorbed depreciation can be carried forward indefinitely. However, one essential condition for setting off business losses following a transfer is the shareholding continuity test. Under this test, the beneficial ownership of shares carrying at least 51% of the voting power must be the same at the end of both the year during which the loss was incurred and the year during which the loss is proposed to be offset. This test only applies to business losses (not unabsorbed depreciation) and to unlisted companies (in which the public is not substantially interested).

5.13 Transfer Taxes

[63] Securities Transactions Tax is imposed on purchases and sales of equity shares listed on a recognized stock exchange in India at 0.1% of the consideration paid. Securities Transactions Tax is payable both by the buyer and the seller on the turnover (which is a product of the number of shares bought/sold and the price per share). Transfers of shares (other than those in de-materialized form, which are normally traded outside the stock exchanges) are subject to stamp duty at the rate of 0.25% of the market value of the shares transferred.

5.14 Tax Clearances

[64] In cases where proceedings for unpaid tax are pending against the transferor, and where the transferee has acquired the business for inadequate consideration, the tax authorities have been empowered to satisfy the unpaid tax by collecting the remaining balance of the proceeds which ought to have been paid. However, the transferee can avoid difficulties of this sort if:

(1) It insists that the transferor company obtains a 'no objection certificate' ('NOC') from the Income Tax Department to confirm that such transaction is straight (i.e., for an adequate consideration).
(2) It can seek an advance ruling from the 'Authorities for Advance Rulings of India' if it is not sure about the appropriate tax treatment.

6 TYPES OF COMPANIES AND INCORPORATION UNDER THE COMPANIES ACT, 2013

6.1 Distinction of Companies

[65] Under the Companies Act, 2013 ('the 2013 Act'), companies can be broadly divided into the following three categories:

(1) Public Limited Companies.
(2) Private Limited Companies.
(3) One Person Companies ('OPCs').

6.2 Sub-categories of Companies

[66] The above categories can further be sub-divided into the following sub-categories;

Public Limited Companies

(1) Public Company limited by shares.
(2) Public Company limited by guarantee having a share capital.
(3) Public Company limited by guarantee and having no share capital.
(4) Public unlimited Company having a share capital.
(5) Public unlimited Company not having a share capital.

Private Limited Companies

(1) Private Company limited by shares.
(2) Private Company limited by guarantee having a share capital.

(3) Private Company limited by guarantee and having no share capital.
(4) Private unlimited Company having a share capital.
(5) Private unlimited Company not having a share capital.

One Person Company

(1) OPC Company limited by shares.
(2) OPC Company limited by guarantee having a share capital.
(3) OPC Company limited by guarantee and having no share capital.
(4) OPC unlimited Company having a share capital.
(5) OPC unlimited Company not having a share capital.

6.3 Private Company: Section 2(68), Companies Act, 2013

[67] A *'Private Company'* as defined under section 2(68) of the 2013 Act means a company having a minimum paid-up share capital as may be prescribed, and which by its articles:

(1) restricts the right to transfer its shares;
(2) except in the case of an OPC limits the number of its members to 200;

provided that where two or more persons hold one or more shares in a company jointly, they shall, for the purposes of this clause, be treated as a single member.

Provided further that:

(a) persons who are in the employment of the company, and
(b) persons who, having been formerly in the employment of the company, were members of the company while in that employment and have continued to be members after the employment ceased, shall not be included in the number of members;
(c) prohibits any invitation to the public to subscribe to any securities of the company.

6.4 Public Company: Section 2(71), Companies Act, 2013

[68] A *'Public Company'* as defined under section 2(71) of the 2013 Act and means a company which:

(1) Is not a private company.
(2) Has a minimum paid-up share capital as may be prescribed:

> Provided that a company which is a subsidiary of a company, not being a private company, shall be deemed to be a public company for the purposes of [the] Act even where such subsidiary company continues to be a private company in its articles.

6.5 OPC Section 2(62), Companies Act, 2013

[69] An *'OPC,'* as defined under section 2(62) of the 2013 Act, means a company that has only one person as a member.

6.6 Comparison Between Private and Public Company

[70] The summary table set out below compares the main differences between a Private Company and a Public Company under the Companies Act, 2013.

S. No.	*Section*	*Brief Description*	*Private Limited Company*	*Public Limited Company*
1	2	Meaning	*Right to transfer the shares:* Restricted	A subsidiary of a Public Company is deemed to be a Public Limited Company.
2	2	Small Company	If Paid-up Share Capital does not exceed INR5 m (INR50 lakhs) or such higher as may be prescribed which shall not be more than INR10 crore and turnover as per profit and loss account for the immediately preceding financial year does not exceed INR2 crore or such higher amount as may be prescribed which shall not be more than INR100 crore	Not Applicable

S. No.	*Section*	*Brief Description*	*Private Limited Company*	*Public Limited Company*
3	3	Minimum Members	Two	Seven
4.	3	Maximum Members	Maximum 200	No Limit
5	5	Provision of retrenchment (forced lay-off) in the Articles of Association	To be agreed and approved by all the members	To be agreed and approved through a Special Resolution
6	23	Issue of Securities	By way of Right Issue or Bonus Issue Through Private Placement	To Public through Prospectus ('Public Offer') By way of Rights Issue or Bonus Issue through Private Placement
6	29	Public Offer to be in De-materialized Form	Not Applicable	In case of Public Offer of securities, the securities have to be in Demat Form
7	40	Securities in Public Offer to be listed in Stock exchanges	Not Applicable	Securities offered in Public Offer, to be listed in Recognized Stock Exchanges
8	67	financial assistance and Purchase of Own Shares	Not Applicable	Not allowed to purchase its own shares. No Financial assistance to be given to purchase its own shares

S. No.	*Section*	*Brief Description*	*Private Limited Company*	*Public Limited Company*
9	73	Acceptance of Deposits	Not allowed to accept Deposits from Public	Allowed if Paid-up share capital is INR1 000 m or more; or Turnover of INR5 000 m or more
10	103	Quorum for Meetings	Two members personally present	Five in case of Members up to 1 000; Fifteen in case of Members more than 1 000 to 5 000; Thirty in case of Members exceeding 5 000.
11	138	Internal Audit	Applicable in cases where; 1. Turnover is INR200 crore or more in the preceding financial year, OR 2. Loans from a bank or is more than INR100 crore or more in the preceding financial year	Applicable in cases for all unlisted public companies where; 1. Paid-up Capital is INR50 crore or more in the preceding financial year, OR 2. Turnover is INR2 000 or more in the preceding financial year, OR

S. No.	*Section*	*Brief Description*	*Private Limited Company*	*Public Limited Company*
				3. Loans from banks or NBFCs is INR100 crore or more in the preceding financial year, OR 4. Public deposits are INR250 m or more in the preceding financial year.
12	134(3)(p)	Annual Evaluation in the Board's Report	Not Applicable	If Paid-up share capital is INR250 m or more, details of annual evaluation to be included in the Board's Report
13	139(2)	Rotation of Auditor	Applicable in cases where Paid-up Capital is INR200 m or more	Applicable in cases where Paid-up Capital is INR100 m or more
14	149	No. of Directors and Independent Directors	Minimum Two Not required to appoint an independent director	Minimum Three In the case of Listed Companies, at least one-third must be independent directors
15	152	Retirement by rotation – Appointment of Director	Not Applicable	At least two-thirds of the total number of directors are liable to retire by rotation and eligible to be re-appointed at AGM

S. No.	*Section*	*Brief Description*	*Private Limited Company*	*Public Limited Company*
16	190	Contract of Employment with Managing Director/ Whole Time Director	Not Required (Optional)	Mandatory Provision
17	197	Restriction on Managerial Remuneration	No restriction on the amount of managerial remuneration	Managerial Remuneration is restricted to; 11% of Net profit (subject to conditions); OR at least INR30 lakhs p.a. depending upon effective capital (at least INR60 lakhs Per Annum as per Schedule V of the Companies Act, 2013)

7 FOREIGN INVESTMENT IN INDIA/ALLOTMENT OF SHARES/REPORTING

7.1 Who Can Invest in India?

[71] A non-resident entity can invest in India, subject to the FDI Policy, except in those sectors/activities which are prohibited. However, investments from an entity in a country that shares a land border with India will require government approval. An entity of a country, which shares a land border with India or where the beneficial owner of an investment into India is situated in or is a citizen of any such country, can invest only under the Government route. Further, a citizen of Pakistan or an entity incorporated in Pakistan can invest, only under the Government route, in sectors/activities other than defence, space, atomic energy and sectors/activities prohibited for foreign investment.

7.2 Entities into Which FDI Can Be Made

[72] This section describes the entities into which FDI can be made:

(1) FDI in an Indian Company:
Indian companies can issue capital against FDI.
(2) FDI in a Partnership Firm/Proprietary Concern:
(a) A Non-Resident Indian (NRI) or a Person of Indian Origin (PIO) resident outside India can invest in the capital of a firm or of a proprietary concern in India on a non-repatriation basis provided:
(i) The amount is invested by inward remittance or out of an NRE/FCNR (B)/NRO account maintained with Authorized Dealers/Authorized Banks.
(ii) The firm or proprietary concern is not engaged in any agricultural/plantation or real estate business or print media sector.
(iii) The amount invested is not eligible for repatriation outside India.
(b) Investments with repatriation option: NRIs/PIO may seek prior permission from the Reserve Bank for investment in sole proprietorship concerns/partnership firms with a repatriation option. The application will be decided in consultation with the Government of India.
(c) Investment by non-residents other than NRIs/PIO: A person resident outside India other than NRIs/PIO may make an application and seek prior approval of the Reserve Bank to make an investment in the capital of a firm or a proprietorship concern or any association of persons in India. The application will be decided in consultation with the Government of India.
(d) Restrictions: An NRI or PIO is not allowed to invest in a firm or proprietorship concern engaged in any agricultural/plantation activity or real estate business or print media.

7.3 Types of Instruments

[73] This section describes the types of instruments that may be issued by Indian companies:

(1) Indian companies can issue equity shares, fully and mandatorily convertible debentures, and fully and mandatorily convertible preference shares subject to pricing guidelines/valuation norms prescribed under FEMA Regulations. The price/conversion formula of convertible capital instruments should be determined upfront at the time of issue of the relevant instruments. The price at the time of conversion should not, in any case, be

lower than the fair value established, at the time of issuance of such instruments, in accordance with the extant FEMA regulations [as per any internationally accepted pricing methodology on an arm's length basis for unlisted companies, and as per valuation carried out in terms of the SEBI (ICDR) Regulations, for listed companies].

(2) Optionality clauses are allowed in equity shares, fully and mandatorily convertible debentures and fully and mandatorily convertible preference shares under the FDI scheme, subject to the following conditions:
  (a) There is a minimum lock-in period of one year taking effect from the date of allotment of such capital instruments.
  (b) After the lock-in period and subject to FDI Policy provisions (if any), the non-resident investor exercising the option/right is eligible to exit without any assured return, as per the pricing/valuation guidelines issued by [RBI] from time to time.

(3) Other types of preference shares/debentures (i.e., non-convertible, optionally convertible or partially convertible preference shares/debentures, for which funds were received on or after 1 May 2007) are considered debt. Accordingly, all norms applicable for External Commercial Borrowings (ECBs) relating to eligible borrowers, recognized lenders, amount and maturity, end-use stipulations, etc., will apply. Since these instruments would be denominated in rupees, the rupee interest rate would be based on the swap equivalent of the London Interbank Offered Rate plus the spread as permissible for ECBs of corresponding maturity.

(4) The inward remittance received by the Indian company vides issuance of Depository Receipts (DRs) and Foreign Currency Convertible Bonds (FCCB) are treated as FDI and counted towards FDI.

7.4 Issue/Transfer of Shares

7.4.1 Issuance of Shares

[74] The capital instruments should be issued within 180 days from the date of receipt of the inward remittance received through normal banking channels, including any escrow account opened and maintained for the purpose, or by debit to the NRE/FCNR (B) account of the non-resident investor. If the capital instruments are not issued within 180 days from the date of receipt of the inward remittance or date of debit to the NRE/FCNR (B) account, the amount of consideration so received should be refunded immediately to the non-resident investor by outward remittance through normal banking channels or by a credit to the NRE/FCNR (B) account, as the case may be. Non-compliance with the above provision would be regarded as a contravention under FEMA and would attract penal provisions. In exceptional cases, a refund of any consideration outstanding beyond a period of 180 days from the date of receipt may be considered by the RBI, depending on the merits of the case.

7.4.2 Issue Price of Shares

[75] The price of shares issued to persons resident outside India under the FDI Policy, must not be less than:

(a) the price calculated in accordance with the Securities and Exchange Board of India ('SEBI') guidelines, as applicable, where the shares of the company are listed on any recognized stock exchange in India;
(b) the fair valuation of such shares as determined by a SEBI registered Merchant Banker or Chartered Accountant in accordance with any internationally accepted pricing methodology on an arm's length basis, where the shares of the company are not listed on any recognized stock exchange in India; and
(c) The price is applicable to the transfer of shares from resident to non-resident as per the pricing guidelines laid down by the Reserve Bank from time to time, where the issue of the shares is by way of preferential allotment.

[76] However, where non-residents (including NRIs) are making investments in an Indian company in compliance with the provisions of the Companies Act, as applicable, by way of subscription to its Memorandum of Association, such investments may be made at face value subject to their eligibility to invest under the FDI scheme.

7.4.3 Foreign Currency Account

[77] Indian companies which are eligible to issue shares to persons resident outside India under the FDI Policy may be allowed to retain the share subscription proceeds in a Foreign Currency Account, with the prior approval of RBI.

7.4.4 Transfer of Shares and Convertible Debentures

[78] Subject to FDI sectoral policy (relating to sectoral caps and entry routes), applicable laws and other conditions including security conditions, non-resident investors can also invest in Indian companies by purchasing/acquiring existing shares from Indian shareholders or from other non-resident shareholders. General permission has been granted to non-residents/NRIs for the acquisition of shares by way of transfer subject to the following:

(a) A person resident outside India (other than non-residents of India [NRIs] and erstwhile overseas corporate bodies 'OCBs') may transfer shares or convertible debentures by way of sale or gift to any person resident outside India (including NRIs). Government approval is not required for the transfer of shares in the investee company from one non-resident to another non-resident in sectors that are under the Automatic Route. In addition, Government approval will be required for the transfer of a stake from one non-resident to another non-resident in sectors that are under the Government approval route.

(b) NRIs may transfer shares or convertible debentures held by them to another NRI by way of sale or gift.
(c) A person resident outside India can transfer any security to a person resident in India by way of gift.
(d) A person resident outside India can transfer shares and convertible debentures of an Indian company listed on a recognized Stock Exchange in India through a stockbroker registered with a stock exchange or a merchant banker registered with SEBI.
(e) A person resident in India can transfer, by way of sale, shares (including subscriber shares) or convertible debentures of an Indian company under private arrangement to a person resident outside India, subject to certain guidelines.
(f) General permission is also available for the transfer of shares/convertible debentures, by way of sale under private arrangement, by a person resident outside India to a person resident in India, subject to certain guidelines.
(g) The above General Permission also covers the transfer by a resident to a non-resident of shares/convertible debentures of an Indian company which is engaged in an activity previously covered under the Government Route but now falling under the Automatic Route, as well as the transfer of shares by a non-resident to an Indian company under a buyback and/or capital reduction scheme of the company.
(h) FC-TRS should be submitted to the AD Category-I Bank, within sixty days from the date of receipt of the amount of consideration. The onus of submission of the Form FC-TRS within the given timeframe falls on the transferor/transferee, resident in India. However, in cases where the NR investor, including an NRI, acquires shares on the stock exchanges under the FDI scheme, the investee company would have to file the form FC-TRS with the AD Category-I bank.
(i) The sale consideration in respect of equity instruments purchased by a person resident outside India remitted into India through normal banking channels, has to be subjected to a Know Your Customer (KYC) check by the remittance-receiving AD Category-I bank at the time of receipt of funds. If the remittance-receiving AD Category-I bank is different from the AD Category-I bank handling the transfer transaction, the KYC check should be carried out by the remittance-receiving bank, and the KYC report should be submitted by the customer to the AD Category-I bank carrying out the transaction along with the Form FC-TRS.

7.5 Takeover or Acquisition

[79] A person resident outside India including an NRI investor who has already acquired and continues to maintain control in accordance with the SEBI (SAST) Regulations can acquire shares of a listed Indian company on a stock exchange through a registered broker under the FDI scheme provided that the original and resultant investments are in line with the extant FDI policy and FEMA regulations in respect of sectoral cap, entry route, mode of payment, reporting requirement, documentation, etc.

7.6 Escrow

[80] AD Category-I banks have been given general permission to open escrow accounts and special accounts of non-resident corporates for open offers/exit offers and delisting of shares. The relevant SEBI (SAST) Regulations, 2011 (SAST) Regulations or any other applicable SEBI Regulations/provisions of the Companies Act, will be applicable. AD Category-I banks have also been permitted to open and maintain, without the prior approval of RBI, *non-interest-bearing* escrow accounts in Indian Rupees in India on behalf of residents and/or non-residents, towards payment of share purchase consideration, and/or to provide escrow facilities for keeping securities to facilitate FDI transactions subject to the terms and conditions specified by RBI. SEBI authorized Depository Participants have also been permitted to open and maintain, without the prior approval of RBI, escrow accounts for securities subject to the terms and conditions specified by RBI. In both cases, the escrow agent must necessarily be an AD Category-I bank or SEBI authorized Depository Participant (in case of securities accounts). These facilities will be applicable both for the issue of fresh shares to the non-residents as well as the transfer of existing shares from/to the non-residents.

7.7 Prior Permission of RBI in Certain Cases for Transfer of Capital Instruments

[81] Except for the cases mentioned in sub-paragraph (3) below, the following cases require the prior approval of the RBI:

(1) The transfer of capital instruments from residents to non-residents by way of sale where:
   (a) The transfer is at a price that falls outside the pricing guidelines specified by the Reserve Bank from time to time, and the transaction does not fall under the exception referred to in paragraph (3) below.
   (b) The transfer of capital instruments by the non-resident acquirer involves a deferral of payment of the consideration. Further, where approval is granted for a transaction, the same should be reported in Form FC-TRS to an AD Category-I bank for the necessary due diligence, within sixty days from the date of receipt of the full and final amount of consideration.

(2) The transfer of any capital instrument, by way of gift by a person resident in India to a person resident outside India.

(3) In the following cases, the approval of the RBI is not required:

(a) The transfer of shares from a Non-Resident to a Resident under the FDI scheme where the pricing guidelines under FEMA, 1999 are not met provided that:
   (i) The original and resultant investments are in line with the extant FDI policy and FEMA regulations in terms of sectoral caps, conditions (such as minimum capitalization, etc.), reporting requirements, documentation, etc.
   (ii) The pricing for the transaction is compliant with the specific/explicit, extant and relevant SEBI regulations/guidelines.
   (iii) Where a Chartered Accountant's Certificate confirming compliance with the relevant SEBI regulations/guidelines, as indicated above, is attached to the form FC-TRS to be filed with the Authorized Bank AD bank.

(b) The transfer of shares from a Resident to a Non-Resident where the transfer of shares requires the prior approval of the Government conveyed through Foreign Investment Facilitation Portal (FIFP) (erstwhile Foreign Investment Promotion Board) as per the extant FDI policy provided that:
   (i) the requisite approval of the FIFP has been obtained; and
   (ii) the transfer of shares adheres to the pricing guidelines and documentation requirements specified by the RBI from time to time.

(c) Where the transfer of shares attracts SEBI (SAST) Regulations, subject to adherence with the pricing guidelines and documentation requirements specified by the RBI from time to time.

(d) Where the transfer of shares does not meet the pricing guidelines under the FEMA, 1999 provided that:
   (i) The resultant FDI is in compliance with the extant FDI policy and FEMA regulations in terms of sectoral caps, conditions (such as minimum capitalization, etc.), reporting requirements, documentation, etc.
   (ii) The pricing for the transaction is compliant with the specific/explicit, extant and relevant SEBI regulations/guidelines.
   (iii) Chartered Accountant's certificate to the effect that compliance with the relevant SEBI regulations/guidelines, as indicated above, is attached to the form FC-TRS to be filed with the AD bank.

(e) Where the investee company is in the financial sector provided that:
   (i) Any 'fit and proper/due diligence' requirements as regards the non-resident investor as stipulated by the relevant financial sector regulator, from time to time, have been complied with.
   (ii) The FDI policy and FEMA regulations in terms of sectoral caps, conditions (such as minimum capitalization, pricing, etc.), reporting requirements, documentation, etc., have been complied with.

7.8 Conversion of ECB/Lump Sum Fee/Royalty, Etc., into Equity

[82] These are the rules which apply where shares and other securities are issued in exchange for ECBs, technical know-how and other intellectual property:

(1) Indian companies have been granted general permission for the conversion of ECBs in convertible foreign currency into equity shares or fully and mandatorily convertible preference shares, subject to the following conditions and reporting requirements:
   (a) The activity of the company is covered under the Automatic Route for FDI, or the company has obtained Government approval for foreign equity in the company.
   (b) The foreign equity after conversion of ECB into equity is within the sectoral cap if any.
   (c) The pricing of the shares is in accordance with the provisions of paragraph [75] above.
   (d) Compliance with the requirements prescribed under any other statute and regulation in force.
   (e) The conversion facility is available for ECBs obtained under the Automatic or Government Route and is applicable to ECBs, whether due for payment or not, as well as secured/unsecured loans obtained from non-resident collaborators.

(2) General permission is also available for the issue of shares or preference shares against a lump sum fee for technical know-how, or royalties due for payment, subject to entry route, sectoral cap and pricing guidelines (as per the provisions of paragraph [75] above) and compliance with applicable tax laws. Further, the issue of equity shares against any other funds payable by the investee company, the remittance of which does not require prior permission of the Government of India or RBI under FEMA, 1999 or any rules/regulations framed or directions issued thereunder, is permitted, provided that:
   (a) The equity shares are issued in accordance with the extant FDI guidelines on sectoral caps, pricing guidelines, etc., as amended by the RBI, from time to time.
   (b) The issue of equity shares under this provision is subject to tax laws as applicable to the funds payable, and the conversion to equity should be net of applicable taxes.

(3) The issue of equity shares under the FDI policy is allowed under the Government Route for the following:
   (a) The import of capital goods/machinery/equipment (excluding second-hand machinery) is subject to compliance with the following conditions:
      (i) Any import of capital goods/machinery, etc., made by a resident in India, has to be in accordance with the Export/Import Policy

issued by the Government of India/as defined by DGFT/FEMA provisions relating to imports.
- (ii) The application must clearly indicate the beneficial ownership and identity of the importing company as well as of the overseas entity.
- (iii) Applications complete in all respects, for the conversion of import payables for capital goods into FDI, must be made within 180 days from the date of shipment of the goods.

(b) Pre-operative/pre-incorporation expenses (including payments of rent, etc.) are subject to compliance with the following conditions:
- (i) Submission of Foreign Inward Remittance Certificate (FIRC) for the remittance of funds by the overseas promoters for the expenditure incurred.
- (ii) Verification and certification of the pre-incorporation/pre-operative expenses by the statutory auditor.
- (iii) Payments should be made by the foreign investor to the company directly or through the bank account opened by the foreign investor as provided under FEMA Regulations.
- (iv) Applications complete in all respects, for capitalization, must be made within a period of 180 days from the date of incorporation of the company.

7.9 Acquisition of Shares under a Scheme of Merger/ Demerger/Amalgamation

[83] Mergers/demergers/amalgamations of companies in India are usually governed by an order issued by a competent NCLT on the basis of a Scheme submitted by the companies undergoing merger/demerger/amalgamation. Once the scheme of merger or demerger or amalgamation of two or more Indian companies has been approved by an NCLT in India, the transferee company or new company is allowed to issue shares to the shareholders of the transferor company resident outside India, subject to the conditions that:

(1) The aggregate percentage shareholding of persons resident outside India in the transferee or new company does not exceed the sectoral cap.
(2) The transferor company or the transferee or the new company is not engaged in activities that are prohibited under the FDI policy.

Note: FIFP approval would not be required for mergers and acquisitions taking place in sectors governed by the Automatic Route.

7.10 Entry Routes for Investment

[84] Investments can be made by non-residents in the equity shares, the fully and mandatorily convertible debentures or the fully and mandatorily convertible preference shares of an Indian company, through the Automatic Route or the Government Route. Under the Automatic Route, the non-resident investor or the Indian company does not require any approval from the Government of India for the investment. Under the Government Route, prior approval from the Government of India is required. Proposals for foreign investment under the Government route are considered by FIFP.

7.11 Guidelines

[85] Guidelines for the establishment of Indian companies/transfer of ownership or control of Indian companies, from resident Indian citizens to non-resident entities, in sectors with caps: In sectors/activities with caps, including, *inter alia,* defence production, air transport services, ground handling services, asset reconstruction companies, private sector banking, broadcasting, commodity exchanges, credit information companies, insurance, print media, telecommunications and satellites, Government approval/FIFP approval would be required in all cases where:

(1) An Indian company is being established with foreign investment and is not owned by a resident entity.
(2) An Indian company is being established with foreign investment and is not controlled by a resident entity.
(3) The control of an existing Indian company, currently owned or controlled by resident Indian citizens and Indian companies, which are owned or controlled by resident Indian citizens, will be/is being transferred/passed on to a non-resident entity as a consequence of a transfer of shares and/or a fresh issue of shares to non-resident entities through amalgamation, merger/demerger, acquisition, etc.
(4) The ownership of an existing Indian company, which is currently owned or controlled by resident Indian citizens and of Indian companies, which are owned or controlled by resident Indian citizens, will be/is being transferred/passed on to a non-resident entity as a consequence of a transfer of shares and/or a fresh issue of shares to non-resident entities through amalgamation, merger/demerger, acquisition, etc.
(5) It should be noted that these guidelines will not apply to sectors/activities where there are no foreign investment caps, i.e., where 100% foreign investment is permitted under the Automatic Route.
(6) It should also be noted that foreign investment includes all types of foreign investment, i.e., FDI, investment by FIIs, FPIs, QFIs, NRIs, ADRs, GDRs, FCCB and fully, mandatorily convertible preference shares/debentures, regardless of whether such investments have been made under Schedules 1, 2, 2A, 3, 6 and 8 of FEMA (Transfer or Issue of Securities by Persons Resident Outside India) Regulations.

7.12 Prohibition on Foreign Investment in India

[86] Foreign investment is prohibited in a company/partnership firm/proprietary concern/any other entity (whether incorporated or not) which is engaged or which proposes to engage in any of the following activities:

(1) The business of chit fund.
(2) Nidhi company.
(3) Agricultural or plantation activities. However, 100% FDI in the agriculture sector in India is allowed through the automatic route in the following activities:
   (a) Horticulture, floriculture, apiculture and farming of vegetables and mushrooms.
   (b) Animal husbandry, fish farming, and aquaculture.
   (c) Development of seeds.
   (d) Services related to agriculture and allied sectors.
   In addition, foreign investments up to 100% are allowed through the government route in the tea sector, including tea plantations.
(4) Real estate business or construction of farmhouses.
(5) Trading in TDRs.

[87] It should also be noted that *partnership firms/proprietorship concerns* having *investments in accordance with FEMA regulations* are not allowed to engage in the print media sector. In addition, foreign investment is also prohibited in the following sectors:

(1) Lottery Business, including Government/private lottery, online lotteries, etc.
(2) Gambling and betting, including casinos, etc.
(3) Chit funds (a chit fund is a type of rotating savings and credit association system practised in India and which is often organized informally among friends, relatives or neighbours).
(4) Nidhi companies (which are a type of company in the non-banking sector whose core business is borrowing and lending money between their members – also known as mutual benefit funds).
(5) Trading in TDRs.
(6) Real Estate business or construction of farmhouses.
(7) Manufacture of cigars, cheroots, cigarillos and cigarettes.
(8) Activities/sectors not open to private sector investment such as atomic energy.

8 STATUTES INVOLVED IN M&A TRANSACTIONS

8.1 The Companies Act, 2013

[88] Chapter XV (sections 230–240) of the Companies Act, 2013 (the Act) contains provisions on 'Compromises, Arrangements and Amalgamations'. It covers compromises and arrangements, mergers and amalgamations, corporate debt restructuring, demergers, fast-track mergers for small companies/holding subsidiary companies, cross-border mergers, takeovers, amalgamation of companies in the public interest, etc. The procedural aspects involved, such as the format of the application to be made to the NCLT (the Tribunal), the form of notice and the procedural aspects involved with respect to the substantive law are covered under the Rules made under Chapter XV of the Act.

The scheme of Chapter XV goes as follows:

(1) Sections 230–231 deal with compromises or arrangements.
(2) Section 232 deals with mergers and amalgamations, including demergers.
(3) Section 233 deals with the amalgamation of small companies (also called fast-track mergers).
(4) Section 234 deals with amalgamation with foreign companies (also called cross-border mergers).
(5) Section 235 deals with the acquisition of shares of dissenting shareholders.
(6) Section 236 deals with the purchase of minority shareholdings.
(7) Section 237 deals with the power of the Central Government to provide for the amalgamation of companies in the public interest.
(8) Section 238 deals with the registration of offer schemes involving the transfer of shares.
(9) Section 239 deals with the preservation of books and papers of amalgamated companies.
(10) Section 240 deals with the liability of officers in respect of offences committed prior to mergers, amalgamations, etc.
(11) Reduction of capital.

8.2 The Companies (Compromise, Arrangements and Amalgamations) Rules, 2016

[89] These Rules contain provisions dealing with the procedure for carrying out a scheme of compromise or arrangement, including amalgamation or reconstruction.

8.3 Income Tax Act, 1961

[90] The ITA covers matters such as tax reliefs for amalgamating/amalgamated companies, for the carry forward of losses, exemptions from capital gains tax, etc. For example, when a scheme of merger or demerger involves the merger of a loss-making company or the hiving off of a loss-making division, it is necessary to check the relevant provisions of the Income Tax Act and the Rules for the purpose of ensuring, *inter alia*, the ability to carry forward the accumulated losses and to set off such losses against the profits of the transferor company.

8.4 Listing Agreement

[91] Under Regulation 37 of the Securities and Exchange Board of India (Listing Obligations and Disclosure Requirements) Regulations, 2015 where the scheme of merger or demerger involves a listed company, it is necessary to send a copy of the scheme to the stock exchange(s) where the shares of the said company are listed in order to obtain their NOC. Generally, stock exchanges raise several queries, and on being satisfied that the scheme does not violate any securities laws, such as the Takeover Code or the SEBI (ICDR) Regulations, stock exchanges grant their approval. The listed entity must place the Observation letter or No objection letter of the stock exchange(s) before the Tribunal at the time of seeking approval of the scheme of arrangement. The validity of the No objection letter of stock exchanges expires six months from the date of issuance, within which period the draft scheme of arrangement has to be submitted to the Tribunal. Where the shares are listed on BSE or NSE, other Stock Exchanges wait for approval by BSE or NSE before granting their approval.

8.5 Indian Stamp Act and States Stamp Acts

[92] It is necessary to refer to the Stamp Act to check the stamp duty payable on the transfer of an undertaking through a merger or demerger.

8.6 Competition Act, 2002

[93] The provisions of the Competition Act and of the Competition Commission of India (CCI) (Procedure in regard to the Transaction of Business relating to Combinations) Regulations, 2011 must be complied with.

8.7 Approvals of Schemes of Merger

8.7.1 Board of Directors

[94] The first step in carrying out an amalgamation is the approval of the scheme of amalgamation by the boards of both the companies involved. The board resolution should, besides approving the scheme, authorize a Director/Company Secretary or other officers to make an application to the NCLT, sign the application and other documents, and do everything necessary or expedient in connection therewith, including any changes to the scheme.

8.7.2 Shareholders' Members' and Creditors' Meetings

[95] Approval of the scheme of amalgamation is a *sine qua non* for the NCLT's sanction. Without that, the NCLT cannot proceed. Such approval must be obtained at specially convened meetings held in accordance with the NCLT directions [section 230(1)]. However, the NCLT may dispense with meetings of members/creditors. Normally, creditors' meetings are dispensed with subject to certain conditions. (As per section 230(9): the Tribunal may dispense with the calling of a meeting of creditors or class of creditors where such creditors or class of creditors, representing at least 90% by way of value, agree and confirm, by way of affidavit, to the scheme of compromise or arrangement.) For instance, members' meetings may be dispensed with if the individual consent of all the members is obtained.

8.7.3 Stock Exchange

[96] In accordance with Clause 24(f) of the Listing Agreement, all listed companies are required to file the scheme of merger or amalgamation with all the stock exchanges where they are listed at least one month prior to filing it with the NCLT and obtaining its NOC to the scheme.

8.7.4 Financial Institutions

[97] The approval of the relevant financial institutions, including trustees to the debenture holders and banks or investment corporations would be required if the company has borrowed funds either as term loans or as working capital requirements, and/or has issued debentures to the public and has appointed any such financial institution as trustees to the debenture holders.

8.7.5 Land Holders

[98] If the land on which a factory or office is situated is leasehold land and the terms of the lease deed, so specify, approval from the lessor will be required.

8.7.6 National Company Law Tribunal

[99] Both companies (amalgamating as well as amalgamated) involved in a scheme of compromise or arrangement or reconstruction or amalgamation are required to seek approval of the relevant NCLT for sanctioning the scheme. If the transferor and transferee companies are under the jurisdiction of different NCLTs, separate approvals are necessary.

8.7.7 Reserve Bank of India

[100] Where the scheme of amalgamation envisages an issue of shares or a cash option to NRIs, the amalgamated company is required to obtain permission from the RBI subject to conditions prescribed by the Foreign Exchange Management (Transfer or Issue of Security by a Person Resident outside India) Regulations, 2000.

8.7.8 Competition Commission of India

[101] The provisions relating to the regulation of combinations set out in sections 5 and 6 of the CA would also have to be complied with by companies, if applicable.

Process of Merger and Amalgamation-Flow Chart

Check whether Memorandum authorizes Merger

Convene a preliminary Board Meeting

Prepare evaluation report and swap ratio

Prepare a scheme of Amalgamation

Inform Stock Exchange before meeting and outcome of the meeting

Application to the Tribunal seeking direction to call General Meeting/ Creditors Meeting

Convene General Meeting

Convene General Meeting

Reporting results of the meeting to the relevant Tribunal

Obtaining tribunal order sanctioning scheme

Filing copy of tribunal order with ROC

Transfer of assets and liabilities

Listing of shares at the Stock Exchange

Allotment of shares to shareholders of Transferor Company

Post-merger integration

9 INCOME TAX IMPLICATIONS IN CASE OF MERGER

9.1 Role of Income Tax: Status of Two Entities

[102] The impact of income tax is an important factor in deciding on the merger of two or more entities. Relevant considerations may include unabsorbed depreciation, carried forward losses, capital gains, amortization of capital expenditure, etc. The following provisions of the ITA should be considered thoroughly.

9.2 Meaning of Amalgamation

[103] 'Amalgamation' as defined under section 2(1B) of the ITA means, in relation to companies, the merger of one or more companies with another company or the merger of two or more companies to form one company (the company or companies which so merge being referred to as the amalgamating company or companies and the company with which they merge or which is formed as a result of the merger, as the amalgamated company), in such a manner that:

(1) All the property of the amalgamating company or companies immediately before the amalgamation becomes the property of the amalgamated company by virtue of the amalgamation.
(2) All the liabilities of the amalgamating company or companies immediately before the amalgamation become the liabilities of the amalgamated company by virtue of the amalgamation.
(3) Shareholders holding not less than three-fourths in value of the shares in the amalgamating company or companies (other than shares already held therein immediately before the amalgamation by, or by a nominee for, the amalgamated company or its subsidiary) become shareholders of the amalgamated company by virtue of the amalgamation, otherwise than as a result of the acquisition of the property of one company by another company pursuant to the purchase of such property by the other company or as a result of the distribution of such property to the other company after the winding up of the first-mentioned company.

Thus, for a merger to qualify as an 'amalgamation' for the purpose of the Income Tax Act, the above three conditions have to be satisfied.

9.3 Provisions of the Income Tax Act, 1961 Which Are Vital in Deciding Between Merger with or Acquisition of Target Company

[104] The following provisions of the ITA are vital in deciding whether to merge with the target company or acquire the target company.

Section 79: Carry forward and set off losses in the case of certain companies

Where a change in shareholding has taken place in a previous year in the case of a company, not being a company in which the public is substantially interested, no loss incurred in any year prior to the previous year shall be carried forward and set off against the income of the previous year unless on the last day of the previous year shares of the company carrying not less than 51% of the voting power were beneficially held by persons who beneficially held shares of the company carrying not less than 51% of the voting power on the last day of the year or years in which the loss was incurred.

Section 80IA: Deductions in respect of profits and gains from industrial undertakings or enterprises engaged in infrastructure development, etc.

(a) *80IA(12)*: Where any undertaking of an Indian company which is entitled to the deduction under this section is transferred, before the expiry of the period specified in this section, to another Indian company in a scheme of amalgamation or demerger:

(i) no deduction shall be admissible under this section to the amalgamating or the demerged company for the previous year in which the amalgamation or the demerger takes place;
(ii) the provisions of this section shall, as far as may be, apply to the amalgamated or the resulting company as they would have applied to the amalgamating or the demerged company if the amalgamation or demerger had not taken place.

(b) *80IA(12A)*: Nothing contained in above 80IA(12)shall apply to any enterprise or undertaking which is transferred in a scheme of amalgamation or demerger on or after 1 April 2007.

9.4 Certain Deductions to Be on Actual Payment

Section 80IB: Deduction in respect of profits and gains from certain industrial undertakings other than infrastructure development undertakings

(1) *80IB(1)*: Where the total gross income of an assessee includes any profits and gains derived from any business referred to in subsections (3)–(11), (11A) and (11B) (such business being hereinafter referred to as the eligible business), there shall, in accordance with and subject to the provisions of this section, be allowed, in computing the total income of the assessee, a deduction from such profits and gains of an amount equal to such percentage and for such number of assessment years as specified in this section.
(2) *80IB(13)*: The provisions contained in subsection (5) and subsections (7)–(12) of section 80-IA shall, so far as may be, apply to the eligible business under this section.

9.5 Cost with Reference to Certain Modes of Acquisition

Section 80IC: Special provisions in respect of certain undertakings or enterprises in certain special category States

(1) *80IC(1)* Where the total gross income of an assessee includes any profits and gains derived by an undertaking or an enterprise from any business referred to in subsection (2), there shall, in accordance with and subject to the provisions of this section, be allowed, in computing the total income of the assessee, a deduction from such profits and gains, as specified in subsection (3).
(2) *80IC(17)* The provisions contained in subsection (5) and subsections (7)–(12) of section 80-IA shall, so far as may be, apply to the eligible undertaking or enterprise under this section.

9.6 No Capital Gain

Section 47(via) In respect of any transfer, in a scheme of amalgamation, of shares held in an Indian company, by the amalgamating foreign company to the amalgamated foreign company, there is no capital gain if the following conditions are satisfied:

(a) at least 25% of the shareholders of the amalgamating foreign company continue to remain shareholders of the amalgamated foreign company; and
(b) such transfer does not attract tax on capital gains in the country in which the amalgamating company is incorporated.

Section 47(vicc): In respect of any transfer, in a scheme of amalgamation, of a capital asset, being a share of a foreign company [referred to in explanation 5 to clause (i) of subsection (1) of section 9], which derives, directly or indirectly, its value substantially from the share or shares of an Indian company, held by the amalgamating foreign company to the amalgamated foreign company if:

(a) at least 25% of the shareholders of the amalgamating foreign company continue to remain shareholders of the amalgamated foreign company; and
(b) such transfer does not attract tax on capital gains in the country in which the amalgamating company is incorporated.

10 DEMERGER

10.1 Definition and Introduction

[105] The word demerger has been defined in section 2(19AA) of the ITA as follows:

> 'demerger,' in relation to companies, means the transfer, pursuant to a scheme of arrangement under sections 391 to 394 of the Companies Act, 1956 by a demerged company of one or more of its undertakings to any resulting company in such a manner that:
>
> (1) All the property of the undertaking being transferred by the demerged company, immediately before the demerger, becomes the property of the resulting company by virtue of the demerger.
> (2) All the liabilities relating to the undertaking being transferred by the demerged company, immediately before the demerger, become the liabilities of the resulting company by virtue of the demerger.
> (3) The property and the liabilities of the undertaking or undertakings being transferred by the demerger company are transferred at values appearing in its books of account immediately before the demerger.

(4) The resulting company issues, in consideration of the demerger, its shares to the shareholders of the demerged company on a proportionate basis.
(5) The shareholders holding not less than three-fourths in value of the shares in the demerged company (other than shares already held therein immediately before the demerger, or by a nominee for the resulting company or its subsidiary) become shareholders of the resulting company or companies by virtue of the demerger, otherwise than as a result of the acquisition of the property or assets of the demerged company or any undertaking thereof by the resulting company.
(6) The transfer of the undertaking is on a going concern basis.
(7) The demerger is in accordance with the conditions, if any, notified under subsection (5) of section 72A by the Central Government on this behalf.

10.2 Methods of Demerger

[106] Demerger could be effected in any of the following three ways:

(1) Demerger by agreement between promoters.
(2) Demerger under a scheme of arrangement with the approval of the NCLT under section 230.
(3) Demerger under a voluntary winding up through a liquidator.

10.3 Types of Demergers

10.3.1 Partial Demerger

[107] In a partial demerger, one of the undertakings or a part of the undertaking or a department or a division of an existing company is separated and transferred to one or more new company/companies, formed with substantially the same shareholders, who are allotted shares in the new company in the same proportion as the separated division, department, etc., bears to the total undertaking of the company.

10.3.2 Complete Demerger

[108] In the case of a partial demerger, the existing company also continues to maintain its separate legal identity, and the new company, a separate legal identity, carries on the separated or spun-off business and undertaking of the existing company.

[109] In a complete demerger, an existing company transfers its various divisions, undertakings, etc., to one or more new companies formed for this purpose. The existing company is then dissolved by passing a special resolution for members' voluntary winding up. The liquidator is also authorized by special resolution to transfer its undertakings, divisions, etc., to one or more companies in accordance with the scheme of demerger approved by the shareholders of the company by a special resolution. The shareholders of the dissolved company are issued and allotted shares in the new company or companies, as the case may be, on the basis of the predetermined shares exchange ratio, in accordance with the scheme of demerger.

[110] In the case of complete demerger, the existing company disappears from the corporate scene. It is voluntarily wound up, and its entire business and undertakings are transferred to one or more new companies.

10.4 Rules and Forms in Respect of a Scheme of Demerger

[111] The procedure for convening, holding and conducting the class meetings required for effecting a demerger, is laid down in the Companies (Compromise, Arrangements and Amalgamations) Rules, 2016.

10.5 Tax Concession/Incentives in Case of Demerger

[112] If any demerger takes place within the meaning of section 2(19AA) of the Income Tax Act, the following tax concessions are available to:

(1) The demerged company.
(2) The shareholders of the demerged company.
(3) The resulting company.

[113] These concessions are on similar lines to those available in cases of amalgamation. However, some concessions available in respect of an amalgamation are not available in respect of a demerger.

10.6 Tax Concessions to Demerged Company

10.6.1 No Capital Gains

[114] Where there is a transfer of any capital asset in the context of demerger by the demerged company to the resulting company, such transfer will not be regarded as a transfer for the purpose of capital gains tax provided the resulting company is an Indian company (as per section 47(vib) of the ITA).

10.6.2 Tax Concession to a Foreign Demerged Company

[115] Where a foreign company holds any shares in an Indian company and transfers the same, in the context of a demerger, to another resulting foreign company, such transaction will not be regarded as a transfer for the purpose of capital gains tax subject to fulfilment of certain conditions such as:

(a) at least 75% of the shareholders of the demerged foreign company continue to remain shareholders of the resulting foreign company; and
(b) such transfer does not attract tax on capital gains in the country in which the demerged foreign company is incorporated.

10.6.3 Reserves for Shipping Business

[116] Where a ship, acquired out of the free reserves of the demerged company, is transferred in a scheme of demerger, even within the period of eight years of acquisition, there will be no deemed profits to the demerged company.

10.7 Tax Concessions to Shareholders of the Demerged Company (Section 47 (vi)(d))

10.7.1 No Capital Gain

[117] Any transfer or issue of shares by the resulting company, in a scheme of demerger, to the shareholders of the demerged company will not be regarded as a transfer if the transfer or issue is made in consideration of the demerger of the undertaking.

[118] In the case of a demerger, the existing shareholder of the demerged company will hold after the demerger:

(a) Shares in the resulting company.
(b) Shares in the demerged company.

[119] And if a shareholder transfers any of the above shares subsequent to the demerger, the cost of such shares shall be calculated as set out below in paragraphs [120] & [121].

[120] The cost of acquisition of shares in the resulting company held by the assessee will be the same proportion as the net book value of the assets transferred in the demerger bears to the net worth of the demerged company immediately before such demerger.

[121] The cost of acquisition of the original shares held by the shareholder in the demerged company shall be deemed to have been reduced by the amount as arrived at pursuant to paragraph [121] above.

[122] For the above purpose, 'net worth' shall mean the aggregate of the paid-up share capital and general reserves in the books of account of the demerged company immediately before the demerger.

10.7.2 Period of Holding of Shares of the Resulting Company

[123] In the case of a capital asset, being a share or shares in an Indian company, which become(s) the property of the assessee in consideration of a demerger, there shall be taken into account the period for which the share or shares held in the demerged company were held by the assessee.

[124] In other words, in order to decide whether a long-term capital gain or a short-term capital gain is involved, the holding period of the demerged company must be taken into account.

10.8 Tax Concession to the Resulting Company

[125] The resulting company will be eligible for tax concessions only if the following two conditions are satisfied as stated in paragraph [106] above:

(1) The demerger satisfies all the conditions laid down in section 2(19AA) of the Income Tax Act.
(2) The resulting company is an Indian company.

[126] The following concessions are available to the resulting company pursuant to a scheme of demerger.

10.8.1 Expenditure on Acquisition of Patent Rights or Copyrights

[127] Where patents or copyrights acquired by the demerged company are transferred to any resulting Indian company, the provisions of section 35A, which were applicable to the demerged company, become applicable in the same manner to the resulting company.

10.8.2 Expenditure on Know-How

[128] Where there is a transfer of an undertaking under a scheme of demerger, the resulting company will be entitled to claim a deduction under section 35AB of the Income Tax Act in respect of such undertaking to the same extent and in respect of the same residual period as would have been allowed to the demerger company, had such demerger not taken place.

10.8.3 Expenditure for Obtaining License to Operate Telecommunication Services

[129] Where in a scheme of demerger, the demerged company sells or otherwise transfers its license to the resulting company (being an Indian company), the provisions of section 35ABB of the Income Tax Act which were applicable to the demerged company become applicable in the same manner to the resulting company.

10.8.4 Treatment of Preliminary Expenses

[130] Where the undertaking of an Indian company which is entitled to a deduction of preliminary expenses is transferred before the expiry of ten years or five years, as the case may be, to another company in a scheme of demerger, the preliminary expenses of such undertaking which are not yet written off will be allowed as a deduction to the resulting company in the same manner as would have been allowed to the demerged company in accordance with the provisions of section 35D of the Income Tax Act. The demerged company will not be entitled to the deduction thereafter.

10.8.5 Treatment of Expenditure on Prospecting, Etc., for Certain Minerals

[131] Where the undertaking of an Indian company which is entitled to a deduction on account of prospecting for minerals, is transferred before the expiry of the period of ten years to another company in a scheme of demerger, such expenditure will, to the extent not yet written off, be allowed as a deduction to the resulting company in the same manner as would have been allowed to the demerged company. The demerged company will not be entitled to the deduction thereafter.

10.8.6 Treatment of Bad Debts

[132] Where due to a demerger, the debts of the demerged company have been taken over by the resulting company, and subsequently, any such debt or part of debt becomes bad, then such bad debt will be allowed as a deduction to the resulting company.

10.8.7 Amortization of Expenditure in the Case of a Demerger

[133] Where an assessee, being an Indian company, incurs any expenditure, on or after April 1999, wholly and exclusively for the purposes of the demerger of an undertaking, the assessee will be allowed a deduction of an amount equal to one-fifth of such expenditure for each of the five successive previous years beginning with the year prior to that in which the demerger took place.

10.8.8 Carry Forward and Set Off of Business Losses and Unabsorbed Depreciation of the Demerged Company

[134] Any accumulated losses and unabsorbed depreciation in a demerger should be allowed to be carried forward by the resulting company if these are directly referable to the undertaking proposed to be transferred. Where it is not possible to relate these to the undertaking, such loss and depreciation are apportioned between the demerged company and the resulting company in proportion to the assets coming to the share of each of them as a result of the demerger.

10.8.9 Deduction Available under Section 80-1A (12) or 80-1B (12) of the Income Tax Act

[135] Where an undertaking which is entitled to a deduction under section 80-1A (12)/80-1B (12) is transferred before the expiry of the period of deduction to another Indian company in a scheme of amalgamation or demerger:

(a) no deduction under section 80-1A(12)/80-1B(12) will be available to the demerged company for the year prior to that in which the amalgamation took place;
(b) The provisions of section 80-1A (12)/80-1B (12) will apply to the resulting company in the same manner as they would have applied to the demerged company.

11 REVERSE MERGER: INCOME TAX IMPLICATIONS

11.1 Meaning of Reverse Merger

[136] Unlike in a merger, where two or more companies of a comparable standing combine, in a reverse merger, a relatively financially sound company merges with a financially weak company.

11.2 Provisions for Reverse Mergers

[137] Where there has been an amalgamation of a company owning an industrial undertaking or a ship or a hotel with another company, or an amalgamation of a banking company referred to in section 5(c)of the Banking Regulation Act, 1949 (10 of 1949) with a specified bank, then, notwithstanding anything contained in any other provision of the Income Act, 1961, the accumulated loss and the unabsorbed depreciation of the amalgamating company shall be deemed to be the loss or, as the case may be, the allowance for depreciation of the amalgamated company for the previous year in which the amalgamation was reflected, and other provisions of this Act relating to set off and carry forward of loss and allowance for depreciation shall apply accordingly.

11.3 Salient Features of Reverse Mergers

[138] Salient features of reverse mergers under section 72A of the ITA include:

(1) The amalgamation should be between companies and none of them should be a firm of partners or a sole proprietor. In other words, neither partnership firms nor sole-proprietary concerns can obtain the benefit of tax relief under a section 72A merger.
(2) The companies entering into the amalgamation should be engaged in either industrial activity or shipping business or hotel business with another company or banking business under section 5(c) of the Banking Regulation Act, 1949, or public sector companies engaged in the business of operating aircraft. In other words, the tax relief under section 72A would not be made available to companies engaged in other trading activities or services.
(3) After amalgamation, the 'sick' or 'financially unviable' company survives, and the other income-generating company becomes extinct. In other words, the essential condition to be fulfilled is that the acquiring company will be able to revive or rehabilitate itself, having consumed a healthy company.
(4) In order to qualify for maximum tax relief, one of the merger partners must be financially unviable and have accumulated losses, and the other merger partner must be profit-earning. A company which is financially unviable should be technically sound and potentially viable from a commercial and economic perspective, but financially weak because of financial stringency or lack of financial resources, or its liabilities exceed its assets, and it is on the brink of insolvency. The second requisite qualification associated with financial unviability is the accumulation of losses for the past few years.
(5) The amalgamation should be in the public interest, i.e., it should not be against public policy, it should not defeat the basic tenets of law, and it must safeguard the interests of employees, consumers, customers, creditors and shareholders (apart from the promoters of the company) through the revival of the company.
(6) The merger should result in the following benefits to the amalgamated (acquired/target) company, viz: (a) the carry forward of accumulated business losses of the amalgamating company; (b) the carry forward of unabsorbed depreciation of the amalgamating company; and (c) the accumulated losses would be allowed for carry forward and set off for eight subsequent years under section 72A of the ITA. The accumulated loss or, as

the case may be, the allowance for unabsorbed depreciation of the amalgamating company will be deemed to be the loss or, as the case may be, the allowance for unabsorbed depreciation of the amalgamated company for the previous year in which the amalgamation was effected, and other provisions of the Income Tax Act relating to set off and carry forward of loss and allowance for depreciation apply.

(7) Accumulated losses should arise from 'profits and gains from a business or profession' and should not be losses arising under the head of 'capital gains' or 'speculation'.

(8) In order to qualify for a carry forward loss, the provisions of section 72 must not have been contravened.

(9) Similarly, for the carry forward of unabsorbed depreciation, the conditions of section 32 should not have been violated.

(10) The 'Specified Authority' has to be satisfied as to the eligibility of the company for the relief under section 72 of the Income Tax Act. It is only on the recommendation of the specified authority that the Central Government may allow the relief.

(11) The company should make an application to the 'specified authority' for the requisite recommendation of the case to the Central Government for the grant or allowance of the relief.

12 THE COMPETITION LAW OF INDIA

12.1 Introduction

[139] Healthy competition results in better goods and services to consumers, while monopoly and concentration of powers result in the exploitation of consumers in terms of quality as well as finance. The CA provides for the establishment of a Commission – namely the 'CCI' – in order to prevent practices which have an adverse effect on competition, promote and sustain competition in markets, protect the interest of consumers and ensure freedom of trade carried on by other participants in the Indian market.

[140] Under the old regime, i.e., the Monopolies and Restrictive Trade Practices Act ('MRTP'), a threshold of 25% was deemed to constitute a position of strength. However, this limit has been eliminated under the CA, which introduces concepts of the relevant market, relevant geographic market, and relevant product market to determine an abuse of a dominant position. In other words, if a company is a comparatively small entity for the entire market of India but holds a dominant position in a specific territory, the CCI can still intervene.

[141] Provisions of the CA prohibit enterprises from entering into agreements that cause or are likely to cause an 'appreciable adverse effect on competition within the relevant market in India'. Under the new regime, the CCI has investigative powers in relation to combinations. Various factors are provided for determining whether a combination will or is likely to have an appreciable adverse effect on competition in India, and penalties are provided for such violations.

12.2 Combination

[142] 'Combination' means the acquisition of control over shares, voting rights or assets, or the acquisition of control by a person over an enterprise where such person already has control over another enterprise engaged in a competing business. The Act is applicable to mergers and amalgamations between or among enterprises when the combining parties exceed the thresholds set out in the Act. The thresholds are unambiguously specified in the Act in terms of assets or turnover in India and abroad. Entering into a combination that causes or is likely to cause an appreciable adverse effect on competition within the relevant market in India is prohibited and such combination would be void.

12.3 Combinations: Thresholds

[143] The current thresholds for the combined assets/turnover of the combining parties are as follows:

(1) *Individual*: Either the combined assets of the enterprises are more than INR20 bn in India, or the combined turnover of the enterprises is more than INR60 bn in India. If either or both of the enterprises also have assets/turnover outside India, then the Act applies if the combined assets of the enterprises are more than USD1 bn, including at least INR10 bn in India or the combined turnover is more than USD3 bn, including at least INR30 bn in India.
(2) *Group:* The group to which the enterprise would belong post acquisition, whose control, shares, assets or voting rights are being acquired, or the group to which the enterprise remaining after the merger or amalgamation would belong, has either INR80 bn in India or turnover of more than INR240 bn in India. Where the group has a presence in India as well as outside India, then the group has assets of more than USD4 bn, including at least INR10 bn in India or turnover of more than USD12 bn, including at least INR30 bn in India.
(3) The term 'Group' is explained in the Act. Two enterprises belong to a 'Group' if one is in a position to exercise at least 26% of the voting rights, appoint at least 50% of the directors or control the management or affairs of the other. However, the government has exempted 'Groups' exercising less than 50% of the voting rights in another enterprise from the provisions of section 5 of the Act for a period of five years starting from 4 March 2016.
(4) In exercise of the powers conferred by section 54(a) of the CA, the Central Government, in the public interest, exempts from the provisions of section

5 of the said Act, for a period of five years, an enterprise whose control, shares, voting rights or assets are being acquired which has either assets of the value of not more than INR3.5 bn in India or turnover of not more than INR10 bn in India.

12.4 Notice to the Commission Disclosing Details of the Proposed Combination

[144] Section 6 of the Competition Act prohibits any person or enterprise from entering into a combination that causes or is likely to cause an appreciable adverse effect on competition within the relevant market in India and if such a combination is formed, it is void.

[145] Section 6(2) requires that any person or enterprise, who or which proposes to enter into any combination, shall give notice to the Commission disclosing details of the proposed combination, in the form prescribed and submit the form together with the fee prescribed by regulations. Such intimation should be submitted within thirty days of:

(1) Approval of the proposal relating to the merger or amalgamation, [referred to in section 5(c) of CA] by the board of directors of the enterprise concerned with such merger or amalgamation, as the case may be.
(2) Execution of any agreement or other document for the acquisition [as referred to in section 5(a)] or for the acquiring of control [as referred to in section 5(b) of CA].

13 RIGHTS OF MINORITY SHAREHOLDERS DURING MERGERS/AMALGAMATIONS/TAKEOVERS

[146] In accordance with existing provisions of the Companies Act 2013, approval of the NCLT/Tribunal is required in cases of corporate restructuring (which, *inter alia,* includes mergers/amalgamations, etc.) by a company. The scheme of amalgamation is also required to be approved by shareholders before it is filed with the NCLT. The scheme is circulated to all shareholders for their approval, along with a statutory notice of the NCLT convened meeting together with an explanatory statement under section 393 (Repealed) of the Act.

[147] Though there may not be any protection for any dissenting minority shareholders on this issue, the NCLTs, while approving the scheme, follow a judicious approach by mandating publicity about the proposed scheme in newspapers in order to seek objections, if any, against the scheme from the shareholders. Any interested person (including a minority shareholder) may appear before the NCLT. There have, however, been occasions when shareholders holding insignificant shareholdings, have made frivolous objections against a scheme, with the sole objective of stalling or deferring the implementation of the scheme. The NCLTs have, on a number of occasions, overruled their objections.

[148] It is, therefore, felt that there should be a specific provision in the Act to put a limit (either a minimum number of persons or a minimum percentage of shareholding) for entitling anybody to object to such a scheme. It would also be appropriate to facilitate the acquisition of the remaining 10% of shares in a company, of which 90% has already been acquired by an acquirer. Such acquisition of a residual 10% shareholding should be in accordance with rules to be framed by the Central Government. The Committee has also made recommendations separately, concerning a threshold limit for asserting objections, by barring minority shareholders with an insignificant stake from obstructing schemes of arrangement.

[149] In the case of takeovers, SEBI has powers under the SEBI (SAST) Regulations, 2011 to appoint an investigating officer to undertake an investigation, where complaints are received from the investors, intermediaries or any other person on any matter having a bearing on the relevant allegations. SEBI may also carry out such investigation *suo moto* based on its own knowledge or information about any breach of these regulations. Under section 235 of the Act, a transferee company, which has acquired 90% of the shares of a transferor company through a scheme or contract, is entitled to acquire the shares of the remaining 10% of shareholders. Dissenting shareholders have been provided with an opportunity to approach the NCLT/Tribunal. This scheme of things appears to be fair and should be continued. In order to object to a scheme of amalgamation by investors, a limit should be determined either according to the minimum number of members or according to the minimum percentage of shareholding;

13.1 Existing Legal Provisions of the Companies Act, with Respect to Interest in Mergers/Amalgamation, Etc.

[150] The following provisions of the Companies Act are relevant in respect of interests in mergers and amalgamations:

(1) Sections 230–240 of The Companies Act, 2013 guide the legal procedure for corporate strategies, including mergers, amalgamations and reconstructions.
(2) Sections 230–240, *inter alia,* give the NCLT the power to sanction, enforce and supervise a compromise or arrangement between a company and its creditors/members, subject to certain conditions. These include providing information required by creditors and members of the company concerned before acceding to such an arrangement and facilitating the reconstruction and amalgamation of companies, by making an appropriate application to the NCLT.
(3) Section 235 gives the right to acquire the shares of dissenting shareholders pursuant to a scheme or contract which has been approved by the majority.

Section 237 deals with the powers of the Central Government to provide for an amalgamation of companies in the national interest.

(4) In any scheme of amalgamation, both the amalgamating company and the amalgamated company are required to comply with the requirements specified in sections 230–240 of the Act and to submit the details of all the formalities for consideration of the NCLT.

13.2 Protection of Minority Interest

[151] Section 236 authorizes the NCLT to make provisions for those who dissent from a scheme. Thus, NCLTs have to play a very vital role. It is not only a supervisory role but also a pragmatic role which requires the forming of independent and informed judgment as regards the feasibility or proper working of the scheme and making suitable modifications to the scheme and issuing appropriate directions with that end in view.

14 TAKEOVER

[152] In business, a *takeover* is the purchase of one company (the *target*) by another (the *acquirer*, or *bidder*). Takeover implies the acquisition of control of a company, which is already registered through the purchase or exchange of shares. Takeovers usually take place when shares are acquired or purchased from the shareholders of a company at a specified price in order to secure at least a controlling interest.

[153] Any foreign company wishing to acquire an Indian company has to comply with the laws related to takeover in order to successfully complete the process of acquisition.

[154] Takeover of the management and control of a business enterprise can take place in different ways. The management of a company may be acquired by purchasing a majority stake in the share capital of that company. A company may acquire shares of an unlisted company through what is called an acquisition under sections 235 and 236 of the Companies Act, 2013. Where the shares of the company are closely held by a small number of persons, a takeover may be effected by agreement with the holders of those shares. However, where the shares of a company are widely held by the general public, the transaction will involve the process set out in the SEBI (SAST) Regulations, 2011.

[155] Takeovers may be broadly classified into three kinds:

(1) A '*Friendly Takeover*' means a takeover with the consent of the management of the acquired company. In a friendly takeover, there is an agreement between the respective managements of the two companies through negotiations, and the takeover bid may be with the consent of a majority or all the shareholders of the target company. This kind of takeover is carried

out by negotiation between the two groups. Therefore it is also called a negotiated takeover.

(2) A *'Hostile Takeover'* means a takeover in which an acquiring company may not initially propose an offer to the target company to acquire its undertaking, but unilaterally pursues efforts to gain control against the wishes of existing management.

(3) A *'Bail-Out Takeover'* means a takeover of a financially sick company by a profitable company in order to bail out the former. There are several advantages for a profit-making company to acquire a sick company. The consideration may be attractive to creditors, mostly banks and financial institutions having a charge on the industrial assets, who would like to recover to the extent possible. Banks and other lending financial institutions would evaluate various options, and if there is no other way except to sell the property, they will invite bids. Such a sale could take place in the form of a transfer of shares.

14.1 Legal Aspects of Takeover

[156] The legislation/regulations that mainly govern the conduct of takeover/s are as set out below:

(1) The SEBI (SAST) Regulations 2011.
(2) The Companies Act, 2013.
(3) The Listing Agreement laid down by the relevant stock exchange.

[157] The SEBI (SAST) Regulations 2011 lay down the procedure to be followed by an acquirer for acquiring a majority of the shares or a controlling interest in another company.

[158] As far as the Companies Act is concerned, the provisions of section 186 apply to the acquisition of shares through a company. Sections 235 and 236 of the Companies Act lay down legal requirements for the takeover of an unlisted company by the transfer of the undertaking to another company.

[159] As per Regulation 31A(8) of SEBI (Listing Obligations and Disclosure Requirements) Regulations, 2015, if any public shareholder seeks to re-classify itself as a promoter, such public shareholder is required to make an open offer in accordance with the provisions of SEBI (SAST) Regulations, 2011.

[160] The takeover of a listed company is regulated by clauses 40A and 40B of the Listing Agreement. These clauses in the Listing Agreement seek to regulate takeover activities independently and impose certain requirements of disclosure and transparency.

[161] Sections 391–395 of the Companies Act, 1956 provide a complete code for the merger, amalgamation and takeover of companies.

15 LISTING AGREEMENT WITH THE STOCK EXCHANGES

15.1 Introduction

[162] Mergers, acquisitions, amalgamations and takeovers are important features of corporate restructuring, and the acquirer company can acquire shares of target companies either with the consent of their shareholders or against their wishes. Where the target company is an entity listed on the stock market, then the acquirer has to maintain at least a 25% public shareholding to enjoy continued listing with such stock market.

15.2 Conditions for Continued Listing

Minimum Level of Public Shareholding

Regulation 38 of SEBI (Listing Obligations and Disclosure Requirements) (Regulations, 2015)

The listed entity must comply with the minimum public shareholding requirements specified in Rule 19(2) and Rule 19A of the Securities Contracts (Regulation) Rules, 1957 in the manner specified by the Board from time to time.

Provided that provisions of this regulation shall not apply to entities listed on the [Innovators Growth Platform] without making a public issue.

Regulation 31 of SEBI (Listing Obligations and Disclosure Requirements) (Regulations, 2015)

The listed company agrees that it is a condition for continued listing that whenever a takeover offer is made or a change in a holding pattern, or there is any change in the control of the management of the company, the person who secures the control of the management of the company and the company whose shares have been acquired must comply with the relevant provisions of the SEBI (SAST) Regulations.

16 SEBI (SUBSTANTIAL ACQUISITION OF SHARES AND TAKEOVER) REGULATIONS, 2011

16.1 What Is Acquisition?

[163] An action in which an acquiring company buys all or part of the shares of a target company, such as to assume control of the target company. (As per Regulation 2 (1)(b) of the Securities and Exchange Board of India (Substantial Acquisition of Shares and Takeovers) Regulations, 2011 acquisition means, directly or indirectly, acquiring or agreeing to acquire shares or voting rights in, or control over, a target company).

16.2 Characteristics of Acquisition

[164] Generally, an acquisition is undertaken as a part of a company's growth strategy in circumstances where it is assumed by the acquirer to be more beneficial to take over an existing company's operations rather than to expand its own business. The process of acquisition normally involves a substantial acquirer acquiring a substantial quantity of the shares/voting rights of a target company.

16.3 What Are the Different Types of Acquisition?

16.3.1 Direct Acquisition

[165] A 'direct acquisition' takes place when an acquirer directly acquires shares/voting rights or control of the target company.

16.3.2 Indirect Acquisition

[166] An 'indirect acquisition' is defined as an acquisition of shares or voting rights in, or control over, any company or other entity, that would enable any person and persons acting in concert to exercise or direct the exercise of such percentage of voting rights in, or control over, a target company, as would otherwise attract the obligation to make a public announcement (PA) of an open offer for shares under the SEBI regulations. Accordingly, any acquisition of shares/voting rights or control of a target company consequent upon the acquisition of shares or voting rights or control of another company is an 'indirect acquisition' for the purposes of the Takeover Code. Indirect acquisitions can be categorized into two:

(a) Indirect Acquisition deemed to be Direct Acquisition:
An 'indirect acquisition' is deemed to be a 'direct acquisition' for the purposes of the Takeover Code if the net asset value or sales turnover or market capitalization of the indirectly acquired target company represents more than 80% respectively of the consolidated net asset value or sales turnover or an enterprise value of the directly acquired entity on the basis of the most recent audited annual financial statements.

(b) Indirect Acquisition:
In cases where the above criteria are not fulfilled, then the acquisition is deemed to be an indirect acquisition. In case of an indirect acquisition where the net asset value or sales turnover or market capitalization of the indirectly acquired target company represents more than 15% respectively of the consolidated net asset value or sales turnover or an enterprise value of the directly acquired, the acquirer is under a specific obligation to calculate and disclose a value per share for the shares of the indirectly acquired company.

16.4 Who Is an Acquirer?

[167] Regulation 2(a) defines an acquirer as a person who directly or indirectly acquires or agrees to acquire shares/voting rights/control in the target company either by himself or together with a person or persons acting in concert.

16.5 What Is a Target Company?

[168] A 'target company' includes the following (Regulation 2(z)):

(1) A company.
(2) A body corporate/corporation established under an Act of Parliament/State/Province for the time being in force whose shares are listed on a stock exchange.

16.6 What Are Shares?

[169] A 'share' has been defined to be a unit of the equity share capital of a target company carrying voting rights and includes any security which entitles the holder thereof to exercise voting rights (Regulation 2(v)). For the purpose of this regulation, shares will include all depository receipts carrying an entitlement to exercise voting rights in a target company.

16.7 What Is Control?

[170] 'Control' includes the RIGHT to appoint a majority of the directors or to control the management or policy decisions exercisable by a person or persons acting individually or in concert, directly or indirectly, including by virtue of their shareholding or management rights or shareholders agreements or voting agreements or in any other manner. *Provided* that a director or officer of a target company shall not be considered to be in control over such a target company, merely by virtue of holding such position.

16.8 Who Is a Person Acting in Concert? (PAC)

[171] PACs are persons having a common objective or purpose, who, pursuant to an agreement or understanding, formal or informal, directly or indirectly co-operate for the purpose of acquiring shares or voting rights in, or exercising control over a target company.

16.9 What Is the Maximum Permissible Non-public Shareholding?

[172] The maximum permissible non-public shareholding is 75%, and in accordance with the SEBI Rules, an entity is obligated to bring down its non-public shareholding to the permissible level within a stipulated time.

16.10 What Is the 'Identified Date'?

[173] The 'Identified Date' is the date falling on the tenth working day prior to the commencement of the tendering period for the purposes of determining the shareholders of the target company to whom the letter of offer is to be sent.

16.11 What Is the Offer Period?

[174] The 'Offer Period' is the time period:

(1) between the date of entering into an agreement (formal or informal) to acquire shares, voting rights in, or control over a target company requiring a PA, or the date of PA; and
(2) the date on which the payment of consideration to shareholders who have accepted the open offer is made or the date on which the open offer is withdrawn, as the case may be.

16.12 What Is the Tendering Period?

[175] The 'tendering period' is the time period during which shareholders may tender their shares in acceptance of an open offer to acquire shares made under the regulations.

16.13 How to Calculate 'Enterprise Value'?

[176] The 'enterprise value' is calculated by applying the following formula:

(Market Capitalization of a Company + Debt + Minority Interest + Preferred Shares) – (Total Cash + Cash Equivalents)

16.14 What Are the Different Triggering Points of the Open Offer?

[177] One of the most important obligations under the Takeover Code is the requirement to make an 'open offer' to the public shareholders of the target company upon a substantial acquisition of shares or voting rights or the acquisition of control of the target company, directly or indirectly. The threshold limits for making an open offer are as follows.

16.15 What Is the Trigger Point for a Mandatory Open Offer Obligation on an Acquisition of Shares and Convertible Securities?

Regulation	*Trigger Point*
3(1)	*25% or more of voting rights* – where an acquirer along with persons acting in concert with him acquires 25% or more of the voting rights of the target company he has to make a PA of a public offer for the acquisition of shares of such target company in accordance with these regulations.
3(2)	*Acquisition of additional shares/voting rights amounting to more than 5% of the voting rights over and above the original holding(25% or more of the voting rights but less than the maximum permissible limit)* – An open offer for acquiring shares of such target company in accordance with these regulations. Calculation of the 5% window has to be done on a gross basis regardless of any intermittent fall in shareholding or voting rights, and in the case of issuance of new shares in any given financial year, the difference between the pre-allotment and the post-allotment percentage voting rights will be regarded as the quantum of additional acquisition.
4	*Acquisition of control over the Target Company*

Event	*Trigger Point of Mandatory Open Offer Obligation*
Acquisition of Shares	A mandatory open offer is triggered upon the acquisition of shares that carry voting rights, including any security that entitles the holder thereof to exercise voting rights or the acquisition of voting rights, over and above the thresholds prescribed.

Event	*Trigger Point of Mandatory Open Offer Obligation*
Acquisition of convertible securities	A mandatory open offer is triggered only at the time when these convertible securities are converted.

16.16 What Is the Process of Making an Open Offer?

[178] In the following table, the complete process of making an open offer is explained. Among the steps given, some are compulsory and some are optional, depending on the circumstances.

Action	*Timing*
Appointment of merchant banker	Prior to the PA.
Open Depository Account for shares tendered	Prior to or simultaneous with the PA.
PA	On the date of agreeing to acquire shares or voting rights in, or control over the target company.
Open escrow account deposit consideration	No later than two working days prior to the date of the Detailed Public Statement (DPS). This is as security for performance of acquirer's obligations.
DPS	Not later than five working days after the PA
Filing of draft Letter of Offer 'LOO' with SEBI	Within five working days from the date of the 'DPS' along with non-refundable fee.
Manager to submit a due diligence certificate	This certificate has to be filed with SEBI together with the draft Letter of Offer.
Draft Letter of Offer to be sent to target and Stock Exchange	Simultaneous with submission to SEBI.
Competing Offer	Within fifteen working days of the date of DPS.

Action	*Timing*
SEBI to provide comments on the Letter of Offer	Not later than fifteen working days from the receipt of the draft Letter of Offer, and if no comments are issued within such period, it is deemed that SEBI has no comments. Where clarifications are sought by SEBI: the period for issuance of comments is extended to the fifth working day from the date of receipt of a satisfactory reply to the clarification.
Dispatch of final LOO to the shareholders	Within seven working days of receiving comments from SEBI or where no comments are received, within seven working days from the expiry of fifteen days from the filing of the draft Letter of Offer with SEBI.
Upward revision in number and/or price of shares	Until the last three business days prior to the commencement of the tendering period.
Intimation of upward revision	PA in the same newspapers in which the DPS was published and simultaneous intimation to SEBI, Stock Exchange and the target company.
Comments on the offer by Independent Directors	Within two working days prior to commencement of the tendering period.
Advertisement of schedule of activities	One working day before the commencement of the tendering period. Together with the schedule of activities for the open offer, the status of statutory and other approvals, the procedure for tendering acceptances, etc., to be advertised.
Disclosure of acquisition during the offer period	Disclosure to the Stock Exchange and the target company within twenty-four hours of acquisition.
Commencement of tendering period	Not later than twelve working days from the date of receipt of the comments on draft LOO from SEBI.
Closure of tendering period	Offer has to be kept open for ten working days.
Post offer advertisement	Within five working days after the offer period. Advertisement to be published in a newspaper and sent to SEBI and Stock Exchange, providing details of aggregate number of shares tendered, accepted, and date of payment of consideration.

Action	*Timing*
Open special escrow account	Immediately after closing the tendering period as the acquirer has to complete payment of consideration within ten working days of expiry of the tendering period. Transfer aggregate consideration payable to the special escrow account.
Completion of all obligations by acquirer including payment of consideration	Within ten working days from the last date of the tendering period.
Merchant Banker to release the remaining escrow funds	Within thirty days from the payment of the consideration to the shareholders.

16.17 What Is a Voluntary Open Offer?

[179] Under Regulation 6 of the SEBI (SAST) Regulations, if an acquirer along with persons acting in concert *hold* shares or voting rights in a target company entitling them to exercise at least 25% or more of the voting rights in the target company but less than the maximum permissible non-public shareholding, he is required to make a PA of an open offer to acquire shares of the target company.

[180] A voluntary offer is required for an acquirer to acquire at *least such number of shares* as would entitle the acquirer to exercise an additional 10% of the votes attributable to total shares of the target company.

[181] However, this minimum offer requirement does not apply to any person holding less than 25% of the shares/voting rights in a target company entitling the acquirer to make an open offer for a minimum of 26% of the share capital of the target company.

16.18 What Are the Conditions to Be Complied with in the Case of a Voluntary Offer?

[182]

(1) The acquirer or any PAC with him must not have acquired shares of the target company in the preceding fifty-two weeks without attracting the obligation to make a PA of an open offer.

(2) An acquirer and persons acting in concert with him, who have made a voluntary open offer under Regulation 6 are not entitled to acquire any shares of the target company for a period of six months after completion of the open offer except:
   (a) Pursuant to another voluntary open offer:
      (i) Through bonus issues or stock splits.
      (ii) Through a competing offer.

16.19 What Is a Competing Offer?

[183] The SEBI Takeover Code allows a third party to make an open offer to acquire the shares of the target company when the acquirer's open offer is subsisting. A competitive offer must be made within fifteen working days of the date of the DPS made by the acquirer who has made the first 'PA.' At the same time, it is of prime importance to achieve orderly competition.

The Differences Between a Mandatory Offer and a Voluntary Offer? Sr.No.		*Mandatory Offer*	*Voluntary Offer by Shareholders Holding More than 25% Shares/Voting Rights in the Target Company*
1.	Eligibility of the offer	Compulsory offer to be made by any person triggering the trigger events mentioned below. Can be triggered by direct or indirect acquisitions.	Shareholder in the target company holding shares/ voting rights in excess of 25% but not more than the maximum public shareholding.
2.	Trigger events	Acquisition of shares or voting rights entitling the acquirer and PAC to exercise 25% or more of voting rights in the target company, or	No trigger event. As the name suggests, the offer is made at the absolute discretion of the shareholder.

The Differences Between a Mandatory Offer and a Voluntary Offer? Sr.No.		*Mandatory Offer*	*Voluntary Offer by Shareholders Holding More than 25% Shares/Voting Rights in the Target Company*
		Acquisition of additional shares or voting rights entitling the acquirer and PAC to exercise more than 5% of voting rights in a financial year by an acquirer who together with PAC already holds 25% or more but less than 75% of the capital in the target company, or Acquisition of control over the target company.	
3.	Size of offer	Minimum: 26% of the total shares of the target company. +Maximum: The maximum offer size is linked to maximum permissible non-public shareholding permitted under Securities Contracts (Regulations) Rules, 1957.	Minimum: 10% of the total shares of the target company. Maximum: The maximum offer size is linked to maximum permissible non-public shareholding permitted under Securities Contracts (Regulations) Rules, 1957.

The Differences Between a Mandatory Offer and a Voluntary Offer? Sr.No.		*Mandatory Offer*	*Voluntary Offer by Shareholders Holding More than 25% Shares/Voting Rights in the Target Company*
4.	Revision of offer size	An acquirer may make upward revisions to the number of shares sought to be acquired under the open offer, at any time prior to the commencement of the last three working days before the commencement of the tendering period.	Acquirer is permitted to increase the offer size if there is a competing offer, within a period of fifteen working days from the PA of a competing offer. If there is no competing offer acquirer is permitted to increase the offer size at any time prior to the commencement of the act three working days before the commencement of the tendering period. If the offer size of a voluntary offer is increased on account of a competing offer, then the voluntary offer post such increase shall be deemed to be a mandatory offer under 56 Regulation 3(2).
5.	Other conditions	As detailed herein below	Same as for mandatory open offer. An acquirer may make upward revisions to the offer price at any time prior to the commencement of the last three working days before the commencement of the tendering period.

The Differences Between a Mandatory Offer and a Voluntary Offer? Sr.No.		*Mandatory Offer*	*Voluntary Offer by Shareholders Holding More than 25% Shares/Voting Rights in the Target Company*
6.	Timing and procedure	As detailed herein below	Same as for mandatory open offer
7.	Other conditions	No such conditions	The acquirer or PAC should not have acquired shares of target company without the obligation to make – a mandatory offer during the preceding fifty-two weeks; The acquirer cannot acquire shares of the target company during the offer period otherwise than under the voluntary open offer; acquirer and PAC cannot acquire any shares of the target company for a period of six months after completion of the voluntary open offer except pursuant to another voluntary open offer or competing offer. Exception – Shares acquired through bonus issues or stock splits shall not disentitle the acquirer from making a voluntary open offer.

The Differences Between a Mandatory Offer and a Voluntary Offer? Sr.No.		*Mandatory Offer*	*Voluntary Offer by Shareholders Holding More than 25% Shares/Voting Rights in the Target Company*
8.	Conditional offer	An open offer under the Takeover Code can be conditional on the minimum level of acceptance subject to the following: The agreement resulting in the open offer should contain a condition that in the event the desired level of acceptance of the open offer is not received, the acquirer must not acquire any shares under the open offer or such agreement. The acquirer and PAC must not acquire any shares of the target company during the offer period. Where a conditional offer is made upon a minimum level of acceptance, 100% of the payable consideration in respect of the minimum level of acceptance or 50% of the consideration payable under the open offer, whichever is higher, must be deposited in cash in the escrow account.	Same as in the case of a mandatory offer.

The Differences Between a Mandatory Offer and a Voluntary Offer? Sr.No.		*Mandatory Offer*	*Voluntary Offer by Shareholders Holding More than 25% Shares/Voting Rights in the Target Company*
9.	Withdrawal of offer once made	The general rule under the Takeover Code is that an open offer cannot be withdrawn once the PA is made. However, the following exceptions permit withdrawal of an open offer: (a) The required and already disclosed statutory approvals have been refused. (b) The acquirer, being a natural person, has expired. (c) Any condition stipulated under the agreement triggering the open offer for effecting such agreement has not been met for reasons outside the control of the acquirer. (d) Any such circumstances which, in the opinion of the Board, merit the withdrawal.	Same as in case of a mandatory offer.

16.20 Disclosure Obligations under the Takeover Code

[184] The guiding principle of the Takeover Code is the protection of the interests of the public shareholders of a company. The change in shareholding, voting rights or control of the target company will have a bearing on the interests of the public shareholders. It is important that the target company and the shareholders are not taken by surprise by the shareholding or voting rights of an acquirer and its persons acting in concert. The disclosure obligations under the Takeover Code are provided in Chapter V and are as follows.

16.20.1 Event-Based Disclosure

Regulation	*Made By*	*Trigger*	*Timing*	*Made To*
29(1)	Acquirer	Acquirer + PAC acquiring 5% or more shares of the target company.	Within two working days of the receipt of intimation of allotment of shares, or the acquisition of shares or voting rights.	SE where the shares are listed and the target company.
29(2)	Acquirer	Any person who holds 5% or more of the shares or voting rights of the target company and who acquires, or sells shares representing 2% or more of the voting rights. (Shares taken by way of encumbrance must be treated as acquisition, and on release of such encumbrances, it is a disposal.)		

16.20.2 Continual Disclosure

Regulation	*Made By*	*Trigger*	*Timing*	*Made To*
30(1)	Acquirer	Any Person + PAC holding more than 25% shares or voting rights in the target to disclose their aggregate shareholding and voting rights.	Within seven working days from the financial year ending 31 March every year.	SE where the shares are listed and target company.
30(2)	Promoter	Promoters + PAC to disclose their aggregate shareholding and voting rights.		

16.20.3 Disclosure of Encumbered Shares

Regulation	*Made by*	*Trigger*	*Timing*	*Made To*
31(1)	Promoter	Promoter + PAC pledging or creating encumbrance on the shares of the target company.	Within seven working days from creation, invocation or release of the pledge.	Stock Exchange where the shares are listed and target company.
Reg. 31(2)	Promoter	Invocation or release of the pledge or encumbrance on the shares of the target company.		

17 LABOUR LAWS

[185] Humans, unlike machines, are natural persons and therefore need to be handled with care. Handling the HR of a target company is a complex job due to the labour laws of the land, coupled with the human emotions involved. The labour

laws of India are fairly tilted towards labour due to the socialist nature of the country. HR can be divided into two categories, i.e.:

(1) Workmen, as defined under the Labor laws of India and relevant provisions of the applicable laws must be complied with in respect of them.
(2) Employees other than workmen, who are governed by an employment contract.

[186] In the case of an acquisition of shares, NCLT of laws does not have any role to play. It is purely a contract of sale of securities between the acquirer and the shareholders of the target company.

[187] In the case of a merger, the HR of the target company may object to the scheme of the proposed merger if it adversely affects their working conditions, and in such cases, employees are entitled to a right to a hearing. If the workmen are satisfied that their working conditions in the acquired company would not be inferior to those in the acquiring company, then the scheme of the merger will normally sail through. If not, then the HR must be compensated in accordance with the provisions of the labour laws and the terms of the relevant employment contracts.

[188] If the M&A process involves the transfer of ownership of any undertaking, the new owner or the acquirer has to comply with sections 25F and 25FF of the Industrial Disputes Act, 1947, which are reproduced below.

Section 25F: Conditions precedent to retrenchment of workmen

In accordance with this section, no workman employed in any industry who has been in continuous service for one year or more under an employer shall be retrenched by that employer until:

(1) The workman has been given one month's notice in writing indicating the reasons for retrenchment and the period of notice has expired, or the workman has been paid in lieu of such notice, wages for the period of the notice.
(2) The workman has been paid, at the time of retrenchment, compensation equivalent to fifteen days average pay for every completed year of continuous service, or any part thereof in excess of six months.
(3) Notice in the prescribed manner has been served on the appropriate Government or on such authority as may be specified by the appropriate Government by notification in the Official Gazette.

Section 25FF: Compensation to workmen in case of transfer of undertakings

Where the ownership or management of an undertaking is transferred, whether by agreement or by operation of law, from the employer in relation to that undertaking to a new employer, every workman who has been in continuous service for one year or more in that undertaking immediately before such transfer shall be entitled to notice and compensation in accordance with the provisions of section 25F as if the workman had been retrenched: Provided that nothing in this section shall apply to a workman in any case where there has been a change of employers by reason of the transfer, if:

(1) the service of the workman has not been interrupted by such transfer;
(2) the terms and conditions of service applicable to the workman after such transfer are not in any way less favourable to the workman than those applicable to him immediately before the transfer;
(3) the new employer is, under the terms of such transfer or otherwise, legally liable to pay to the workman, in the event of his retrenchment, compensation on the basis that his service has been continuous and has not been interrupted by the transfer.

18 INSOLVENCY AND BANKRUPTCY CODE, 2016

[189] The old and archaic provisions to deal with sickness arising out of financial difficulties have been replaced by the Insolvency and Bankruptcy Code, 2016 ('IBC'). It is true that business ventures will sometimes fail, and the vision of the new law is to handle such failures rapidly and swiftly, so as to enable promoters and creditors to move on in a timely manner.

[190] The Code consolidates the laws relating to insolvency, liquidation, reorganization of companies, etc. At this point, there are overlapping laws and adjudicating forums dealing with the financial failures of companies and individuals in India. It also amends a number of statutes, including the Companies Act, the SARFAESI Act, the Recovery of Debts Due to Banks and Financial Institutions Act, the SICA Repeal Act, and more.

[191] In the first instance, a corporate insolvency process will be initiated by secured creditors or corporate persons. In rare cases, the process will be initiated by other creditors. This process will last for 180 days, extendable by a further maximum period of 90 days. The resolution professional must file an application to the Adjudicating Authority to extend the period of the corporate insolvency resolution process beyond 180 days if instructed to do so by a resolution passed at a meeting of the Committee of Creditors (COC) by a vote of 66% of the voting shares.

Provided that the corporate insolvency resolution process must be completed within a period of 330 days from the insolvency commencement date, including any extension of the period of corporate insolvency resolution process, which has been granted and the time taken in legal proceedings in relation to such resolution process of the corporate debtor.

Provided also that where the insolvency resolution process of a corporate debtor is pending and has not been completed within the 330-day period referred to above, such resolution process must be completed within a period of 90 days from the date of commencement of the Insolvency and Bankruptcy Code (Amendment) Act, 2019. During this period, efforts will be made to develop a Resolution plan to rehabilitate the ailing corporate by calling upon other operating companies to run the business or even to merge with themselves.

[192] The IBC heralded the departure of the old insolvency practices and laws of India, and for the first time, the definition of an operational creditor was introduced, enabling it to file bankruptcy in case of non-payment of supply of goods or services.

[193] Section 7 of the IBC empowers a financial creditor to initiate corporate insolvency himself or jointly with other financial creditors ('other financial creditors, or any other person on behalf of the financial creditor, as may be notified by the Central Government') against a corporate debtor when a default occurs. The default can also be in respect of any other financial creditor. The application should provide details of the default for the record, and the name of the resolution professional proposed to be appointed as an interim resolution professional.

[194] Section 8 of the IBC empowers operational creditors to initiate corporate insolvency on the occurrence of default, by delivering a demand notice or copy of an invoice demanding payment of the amount involved in the default to the corporate debtor. The corporate debtor is required to reply within ten days of receipt of the copy of the invoice. If he has repaid (paid) the unpaid operational debt, he will notify details of the electronic transfer or encashment of the check issued by the corporate debtor to the operational creditor – section 8(2)(b) of the Insolvency Code, 2016.

[195] Section 10 of the IBC empowers a corporate applicant to initiate a corporate insolvency resolution process with the Adjudicating Authority, where a corporate debtor has committed a default. The corporate applicant must provide, along with the application, information relating to its books of account and such other documents for such period as may be specified, information relating to the resolution professional proposed to be appointed as an interim resolution professional and the special resolution passed by the shareholders of the corporate debtor or the resolution passed by at least three-fourths of the total number of partners of the corporate debtor, as the case may be, approving the filing of the application.

[196] Under section 59 of IBC, a corporate person who intends to liquidate itself voluntarily, and who has not committed any default may initiate voluntary liquidation proceedings under Chapter V Part II of the Insolvency Code, 2016. A company can also liquidate itself voluntarily if a fixed period or event was specified in the Articles of the company for its dissolution. The Voluntary Liquidation of a corporate person shall be allowed subject to such conditions and procedural requirements as may be specified by the Board.

[197] Liquidation, in a nutshell, takes place in the event:

(i) the COC does not agree to a resolution plan;
(ii) the COC decides to liquidate the Corporate Debtor;
(iii) NCLT rejects the resolution proposal;
(iv) if the Corporate Debtor contravenes the resolution plan, the NCLT can pass an order for liquidation of the Corporate Debtor.

[198] Preservation of records: The Liquidator must preserve a physical or an electronic copy of the reports, registers and books of account referred to in Regulations 8 and 10 for at least eight years after the dissolution of the corporate person, either with himself or with an information utility – Regulation 41 of IBBI (Voluntary Liquidation Process) Regulations, 2017.

[199] This Code significantly changes the priority hierarchy for the distribution of liquidation proceeds from that envisaged under the old bankruptcy regime. The distribution hierarchy is subject to the following priorities:

(i) cost of insolvency resolution and liquidation;
(ii) secured creditors, who have relinquished their security enforcement right, and the workers' dues;
(iii) wages and unpaid dues of employees;
(iv) unsecured creditors – financial debt, and so on. Any amount due to the Central Government and the State Government including the amount to be received on account of the Consolidated Fund of India and the Consolidated Fund of a State, if any, in respect of the whole or any part of the period of two years preceding the liquidation commencement date and debts owed to a secured creditor for any amount unpaid following the enforcement of security interest;
(v) any remaining debts and dues;
(vi) preference shareholders if any; and
(vii) equity shareholders or partners, as the case may be.

www.ingramcontent.com/pod-product-compliance
Lightning Source LLC
Chambersburg PA
CBHW071357230926
51846CB00002B/575
9789403526492